PERSONALIZED BEHAVIORAL MODIFICATION:

Practical Techniques for Elementary Educators

by P. Susan Mamchak
with Steven R. Mamchak

Personalized Behavioral Modification bridges the gap between old-fashioned, "punishing" forms of school discipline and the modern theories of Behaviorism which, while interesting from a theoretical standpoint, have little practical value for most elementary educators.

The PBM approach is above all practical and realistic, developed by a former school disciplinarian who had fantastic success working with chronic problem children—the fighters, vandals, underachievers, truants, and disruptors—children who could not be handled by the regular classroom teacher.

Her work demonstrated that outstanding results could be achieved without special theories or equipment, without a specially trained disciplinarian, and without interrupting normal educational processes, either for the disrupter or his classmates. And she gives you all the information you need to implement her system right in this book.

She shows you why and how PBM works in **reality,** not just in theory. She shows you how to set up a PBM program, and how to run it. She shows you successful ways of working with misbehaving children, how to integrate the program with the overall educational goals of the school, how to involve parents and school officials in the program, how to measure the success of the program.

SHOWS YOU EXACTLY WHAT TO DO—STEP-BY-STEP

You are shown what steps to take with each child, from the first incident of misbehavior right through to the point where the causes of his or her misbehavior are rooted out and replaced by more positive, constructive attitudes.

The process for each child may take less than a day, or it may take a year—but in any case it will be a process in which you will encourage and help the child, and keep working toward a goal of enduring attitude and behavior improvement, improvement that will not only help the child cope better in the school environment, but in other

PERSONALIZED BEHAVIORAL

MODIFICATION:

Practical Techniques

for

Elementary Educators

areas of life as well. And this is accomplished **completely within the school,** without any interruption of the child's education.

Mrs. Mamchak does not claim that her PBM Plan can work miracles, nor does she say it can replace the school psychologist. She realizes that some children will not respond ideally to the program, but she believes that it can at least mitigate the disruptive tendencies of such children.

And, because of her long experience, she is fully aware of the problems that can arise with the PBM program; so she covers these potential problems in detail, showing you how to avoid or overcome them.

PERSONALIZED BEHAVIORAL MODIFICATION:
Practical Techniques
for
Elementary Educators

By P. Susan Mamchak
with Steven R. Mamchak

Parker Publishing Company, Inc., West Nyack, N.Y.

Library of Congress Cataloging in Publication Data

Mamchak, P. Susan
   Personalized behavioral modification.

   Includes index.
   1. Individualized instruction. 2. Behavior
modification. I. Mamchak, Steven R., joint
author. II. Title.
LB1031.M33   372.1'1'02   76-10148
ISBN 0-13-657973-6

DEDICATION

To John Naame, M.D., who taught perseverance.
To Donald V. Pease, my father, who taught tolerance.
To Clair W. Bailey, a teacher, who taught pride.
And to Steven R. Mamchak, my husband, who taught
me the most important "behavioral modifer" of all—
love.

ABOUT THE AUTHORS

P. SUSAN MAMCHAK, who is presently President of
PBM Services, developed the PBM program while serving as disciplinarian in Hazlet Township in New Jersey.
Her background in education also includes serving as a
substitute teacher, development of special programs to
raise achievement, and working as a drama teacher.

STEVEN R. MAMCHAK has been a teacher of English and Media for 15 years, and
for much of that time he handled remedial classes. He was chosen to implement
"FOCUS," a program for disaffected children, in Middletown Township, N.J.

How This Book Will Help
Professional Educators. . .

"I had to get rid of him. If he had stayed in my class five more minutes, I'd have hit him!"

"It's so frustrating—I have to suspend him, but I can't help feeling that's exactly what he wants!"

"Day after day, I look out from my office and see four or five kids just sitting there—doing nothing, learning nothing—what a waste!"

Do these statements sound familiar? Certainly, you have heard them repeated over and over on all levels of our educational system. The difficulty in dealing with behavioral problems and classroom disruptors is mirrored in the frustration experienced by teachers and administrators faced with unacceptable or limited options.

You probably have a set of chairs in your school, or perhaps a bench, that is occupied each day with students who must be removed from class. Bravado aside, they are either basically unhappy, scholastically weak, socially unacceptable to all but a small group of their peers, or all of these and more.

What will be done with them? If your school is like most, the choices are restricted. The student can be reprimanded and returned to class, assigned detention or a comparable punishment, held and then returned to class, or suspended from school. Whatever is done, in most cases it is only a matter of time until the student repeats the pattern, the habit if you will, of disruptive behavior; and the removal from class, reprimand by authority, return to class . . . begins all over again. Every experienced educator has bemoaned this depressing, unproductive cycle.

Can anything be done? In light of the measured results of an actual program tested under practical and realistic conditions, the answer is a resounding *"Yes."* The program is called the Personalized Behavioral Modification Plan, and it is what this book is all about.

The PBM Plan is a tested, viable plan whereby the disruptive student is handled *within* the school and continues his education, for he is never removed from the learning process. He gains insight into his behavior and his relationship to others, he is given the tools for changing his behavior, and he receives the personalized reinforcement necessary to *break* his pattern of failure.

Moreover, the PBM Plan requires very little in the form of physical necessities. It can be implemented almost immediately in any school system, and positive results can be realized. It is a plan that has *worked,* and it will work for you.

These statements are the outgrowth of practical experience in the administration of the program. The foundation upon which it is based is time-honored and sound. What makes the Personalized Behavioral Modification Plan unique is its individualized approach which enables each student in the program to feel that it is working for *him.* This personalized factor builds the basis for a change in the behavior of the student.

> • After each visit to the office, Jason was told to "be good." He was told that the vice-principal "didn't want to see him in the office again." To Jason, this meant he had to be a "good boy" from that mid-October day until the close of school in June. Jason knew the impossibility of the task and consequently didn't even try. Under the PBM Plan, if Jason were asked to "be good" he would be told what "good" meant, and it would be "until tomorrow," or at most, "until next Tuesday." Moreover, there would be planned, effective

positive reinforcement and follow-up to insure the success of this "short-term" project. It is upon this success that Jason's future positive behavior pattern would be built.

• Because Debbie always fails spelling tests, she doesn't study for them; and because she doesn't study, she always fails. During the spelling period the day before the test, Debbie's teacher sends her to the PBM room where the PBM Administrator spends the time helping Debbie study for the test. The next day when Debbie takes the test and passes, she is contacted and, on her level of understanding, is shown how she has broken her pattern of failure. Now the Plan begins helping to shape Debbie into a scholastically oriented student.

• The only time Marty gets into trouble is with a substitute teacher. This morning the PBM Administrator checked on teacher attendance and found that Marty's third period teacher was among those absent. Knowing Marty's problem, she sends for Marty during the second period and personally reinforces previous discussions concerning his behavior. A potential trouble spot becomes just another student in the class.

These are a few examples of ideas that have been used in real life situations, but what overall results can you expect by implementing the procedures under the PBM Plan?

Here are just a few:

• A significant drop in the number of suspensions.
• Less and less repetition on the part of chronic disruptors as the pattern of bad behavior is broken.
• The ability to use valuable time for positive, more productive activities.
• An improvement in the educator's image and relationship to the student body as his punitive role ceases to be the major reason for student contact.
• The ability to spot and deal with potential trouble areas *before* they occur, and
• Greater acceptance and participation by parents.

To the teacher, the PBM Plan will create a perceptible, often dramatic change in pupil behavior within the class; a place where a student can receive immediate attention to prevent future unacceptable behavior; an alternative to *direct* punitive action; and a place where work habits may be positively reinforced for low or nonachieving students.

Finally, it will lead to the discovery of positive, new behavioral values by the students. The first offender is given the kind of attention that insures that his behavior does not become repetitive. The chronic offender is given the tools, the guidance and the incentive to *change* his behavior. Each student involved in the Plan finds his work habits improved and begins to build the pattern of success. Moreover, each student develops a sense of self-worth so important to success.

This is the PBM Plan. If you are concerned about the present state of discipline in your school; if you abhor detention, traditional types of reprimand and suspension as punitive options; if you feel there is a correlation between social behavior and academic achievement, then this program is for you. Moreover, if you feel that something can be done—*must* be done, then read on and discover the PBM Plan.

P. Susan Mamchak

ACKNOWLEDGEMENTS

Writing this acknowledgement is almost as difficult as writing the book. Setting down in one page all those who supported this venture is an impossibility. I do think, however, that special mention should be given to those who watched it unfold and lent their support and good wishes.

Nothing as involved as PBM comes to light fully developed; it evolves over several years. Throughout those years, I have had the honor and pleasure of working with educators of the highest caliber. My thanks to the faculties and staffs of Bayshore Jr. High, Thompson Jr. High, Thorne Jr. High, Monmouth Regional High, Shore Regional High, Middletown Township High and Middlebrook Elementary School.

For the understanding, the sharing of experiences and the ideals of education that nurtured the principles of PBM, I wish to thank the following people: Myron Turner, Katy Wells, Grace Jackson-Blake, Phoebe Koontz, Linda Newman, Rose Calcerano-Wachter, Clair W. Bailey and the late Bill Corio.

For their help in the developmental stages of the PBM Plan, special thanks are due to Roman Cabrera, Joyce A. Clark, Kenneth Sheehan and the faculty and staff of Middle Road Elementary School. For their help during the Program's operation, my thanks to Andrea Padlowski, Fred Century and Patrolman Rudy Cherney. For all the seven o'clock nights, noisy Friday afternoons and free time that somehow turned into work periods, a *very* special thanks to you, Teresa "Terry" De Vito and Lavinia "Dinny" Moore-McKee for your loyalty, faith and trust.

This book would have remained only an idea if not for the support and encouragement of Dr. Fred Ball, Dr. Rhoda Anton, Joseph Cole, Elaine Brewer, Jo Matthews, and Ellen Vrabel.

For their support during the actual writing of the book, I must mention those whose opinions, evaluations, commentary and help proved invaluable: Gertrude Woodcock Simpson, Dr. Priscilla Ransohoff, Frank and Greta Singer, Evelyn Yarosh, Florence L. Adair, Shirley A. Johnson, Daniel and Judith Sorkowitz, Kathy Healy, Jacqueline DeBrown, Donna and Kim Ware and Olly Davenport.

Certainly, when talking about those who believed in the concept of Personalized Behavioral Modification, I must give special thanks to Ruth K. Singer who gave up many weekends and brought friends like Betsy "Myrtle" Nichols to work on the outgrowth of the idea that became PBM Services, which could not have been accomplished without Lawrence M. Fuchs, Esq., I. Mark Cohen, Esq., and Roger A. Clapp, Esq.

To Mildred Mamchak a heartfelt "Thanks, Mom!" for the hundreds of cups of coffee, hours of typing and putting up with the rantings and ravings that accompanied the writing of this book.

And how can I fully express the gratitude I have for Steven, my ever-patient, ever-helpful husband. For the hours and hours spent editing and typing, for the painstaking drawing of all the figures in this book, and for always believing—Beloved, I thank you.

Finally, to all the kids in all the schools in which I worked—thanks for making me look good!

P. Susan Mamchak

Contents

1

Understanding Key Factors that Affect Student Behavior

Remember the woodshed? According to some sources that was the place, back in those "good old days," where your father took you when it was reported that you had misbehaved in school and applied a razor strap to the seat of learning! The incident might have been anything from failure to do homework to the unthinkable crime of "sassing" the teacher—the cure was the woodshed expedition.

Today, the razor strap has given way to injector blades, and when was the last time you even *saw* a woodshed? The techniques of yesterday are unthinkable by today's standards, but many of the concerns remain. When the public was asked to list its chief concerns about public education, a recent Harris Poll showed that discipline in the schools resoundly heads the list.

WHY THERE ARE BEHAVIORAL PROBLEMS IN YOUR SCHOOL—AN OVERVIEW

To many outsiders the growth of behavioral problems in the school is something that just happened. The experienced educator, however, is well aware that the increase in behavioral difficulties is neither an overnight nor an inexplicable phenomenon.

How many times have you heard a conversation begin with the words, "Well, when I was in school . . . "? Does an alarm sound? It should, for the person across from you remembers how it used to be, while you know how it is today. Potentially, this is a source of conflict, but it need not be a source of antagonism if both sides are made aware that the school is a viable, constantly changing institution.

Yes, Mrs. A, things were indeed different when you and I were in school. If a child misbehaved as little as 15 or 20 years ago, the punishment he faced at home at least equaled if not surpassed that which the school administered. Moreover, the roles of parent and teacher were well defined, and neither crossed the boundaries of the other. It was the parent's province to feed, clothe, provide health care, and teach manners and discipline while the school's task was viewed primarily as providing education in the basic skills and broadening the student's understanding of the world about him.

Look at the schools of today and you will find lunch programs, free health and dental care, and field trips to places as close as a few miles from the student's home. With the mobile nature of today's society and parents' greater involvement in community and social activities, responsibility has been increasingly delegated and the school has stepped in to fill the need.

Today, people have begun to ask, "Why?" and the student is no exception. "Because I said so" is no longer a valid reason for compliance; no longer can the school dictate such whims as style of dress or length of hair. Corporal punishment has been rightly outlawed, and students seek relevance in what they are taught and in their own relationships with school authorities.

Yes, schools are different today because the world is different today. Values have changed along with society. The student is faced with one set of standards "outside" school, standards advocated or fostered by the media and peer acceptance, and another set "inside," imposed by an often nameless and arbitrary authority. The dichotomy between these two often can be cataclysmic, and the resulting confusion and frustration may well manifest itself in the plethora of behavioral problems facing the school.

CHECKLIST OF PRESENT OPTIONS

When present options for dealing with behavioral problems are examined, it becomes clear that most of them are still based on parental authority. The most punitive option the school possesses is to remand children to their parents for a number of days until they have shown them the error of their ways and have prepared them to return to school. This view of suspension seems antiquated and unrealistic when written, doesn't it? Yet, isn't this exactly what is hoped for when the administration suspends an unruly student? In reality, most educators realize that today suspension is nothing more than a release for students from the school's controls to which they couldn't or didn't choose to conform originally. It is rather like a rabbit being told by the farmer to guard the carrots!

A second group of options is based on the control of teachers and administrators over the "social lives" of their students while they are present in school. Teachers set rules for their classes and if they are broken, punishments are assigned; the punishment, unfortunately, is usually delayed. For example, the smaller students might be told they may not go out on the playground with their class next period. Children are often disturbed and confused when, *an hour after the misconduct,* they can't go out and play. An older child who is told to stay after school may have his misconduct and punishment separated *for hours or even days.*

And what of punishment assignments? Who would not agree with William I. Mackechnie, lecturer in education at Jorden Hill College, Scotland, when he states: "[they] all suffer from a grave disadvantage. If they are not related to some part of the school work, ... they are a waste of time; and, if they are so related, they have the profoundly uneducational effect of connecting these occupations with ... guilt and unpleasantness."[1]

---

[1]Lawrence Stenhouse, ed., *Discipline In Schools, A Symposium* (New York: Perregrin Press), 1957.

The options of the school have been limited both by convention and law. Does the school have the right, for example, to give a student detention without notifying parents or giving students time to change their plans? In one of the schools in which I worked, 24-hour notice was *required*. Can a student be excluded from a gym class? State requirements insist that he must have physical education. The list goes on and on.

No longer can a teacher strike a student. The original removal of corporal punishment, however, has led to extensions that even the founders of the law couldn't have imagined. A student cannot be stood in a corner, placed outside the door of a classroom (with or without a chair) or be given long written assignments, for these may all be construed as corporal punishment. Teachers have to be lawyers, and students know their rights to the letter.

Consequently, it has become evident that without the basis of parental authority, and with the delay between misconduct and punishment and the new "legalism" in the schools, present options are ill equipped to handle present problems.

HOW TO IDENTIFY THE NEED FOR CHANGE

Look around *your* school. How can you pinpoint the places where changes either in options or attitudes are needed? Please understand, this is not intended as a time for self-recrimination; rather, it should be a clear-eyed appraisal of facts in evidence.

When your school opened, how many students did it have? Remember, the physical freedoms permitted in a school of 300 become unthinkable in a school containing 2000 students on double session. Has your student population changed in socioeconomic background, become racially reoriented or more transient due to military or business transfers? How does your school relate to the community? Is there an active PTA? Are school functions well supported? Do the options presently used in your school reflect the attitudes and desires of your community, your faculty and administration, your student body and their parents? Any of these factors affect the personality of a school.

When teachers have been in the classroom for a number of years, class management should not be their main concern. They have a well-stocked "bag of tricks," those little gimmicks that settle the class down to work, take the sting out of a reprimand, or let an "itchy" student know that he has gone too far and now must get in order. But, what happens when the "tricks" don't work as well as you expected?

The need for change manifests itself when one or more teachers find themselves embroiled in almost continuous clashes with their students. No one is wrong, but communication has begun to slow down. Some teachers may be out of step with the changes that have taken place in the school, while some may have difficulty with the downfall of the "magic line," that imaginary wall that supposedly separates the authority of the teacher from the questioning of students.

If you feel that students are worse today than they were five or ten years ago, examine why you think so. Are they "talking back" more? Is the effect of that "little talk" you give the first school day in September losing its punch by the end of October? Are they becoming more destructive of school property? Are the girls, who never gave you a bit of trouble, now "using language that would make a sailor blush"? Do they wear clothes to school that your parents would have burned?

What you are describing are not facts showing that kids have become worse, but that society has changed in terms of values and attitudes. Does that mean you have to tolerate misbehavior? Of course not, but getting the students of today to accept your guidance takes new methods and new options. If you see a need for change, the next step is to start changing.

TAKING A NEW LOOK AT THE "RULES" OF YOUR SCHOOL

When students enter a school for the first time, they are told what is expected of them in terms of behavior. This may be accomplished either by their teacher or by some sort of publication usually entitled "The Student Handbook." During the first few weeks the administrator usually speaks and reinforces what the teachers or handbook has said. To primary students this procedure is adequate—the teacher said they couldn't run in the halls, and so did the principal; there is no question of what is expected. But what of the middle grade students? Their teacher may have told them that the class is expected to line up promptly at the sound of the entry bell, but they may talk quietly while waiting to come in. In a subsequent assembly, however, the principal states that there will be absolutely no talking permitted in the line-up area. Now what do they do? Let's take the students up a few grades and make them sixth, seventh or eighth graders. One rule states that there will be no running in the halls at any time, for any reason, while the next rule declares that any student late to class without a written excuse will be sent to the Office. With the architecture of modern schools and the increased distances between classrooms, walking in the halls may well prevent prompt arrival in class.

Finally, what of the universal rule that states: "Thou Shalt Not Chew Gum In School"? When Ms. Adams tells her class about this rule she adds with a smile, "Of course, if I can't see it or hear it, I can't do anything about it, can I?" Meanwhile across the hall, Ms. Baker finishes with the rule, spots a student with gum 20 feet away and promptly assigns detention! While fortunately not a frequent occurrence, it is illustrative of the type of inconsistency of attitudes often faced by students.

These are just a few examples of inconsistencies, but the list goes on almost indefinitely. The student handbook is a source of even more confusion. Our personal favorite from a handbook is, "There will be no smoking within sight of the school building." Three students were incensed that they were punished for smoking when they were found with their backs against the building, eyes closed, puffing away. After all, in that position they weren't within sight of the building, were they?

These examples are given to show that a new look should

be taken at precisely *what is* acceptable behavior in your school. It is important that you look just at *your* school, for no two are ever alike.

Suppose a girl was running in the halls. Would she be sent to the office, stopped and told to walk to class or ignored? Whatever your answer, *that* is the *real* rule about running in the halls of your school. Suppose a student entered your class a few moments late, but you are still busy with some papers and hadn't started the day's lesson. Would you send him to the office or tell him to sit down and try to be a bit more prompt in the future? Now imagine the same student arriving after you had started teaching. Would you take some punitive action, or ignore him? The point is this: what you really would do is the acceptable behavior you expect, whether it is written that way in the handbook or not.

While going over our records, we became increasingly aware that almost no students had to be reprimanded for breaking a rule that was consistently enforced. Conversely, when a rule was never enforced it caused no difficulties either. Our records show, however, that punitive action constantly took place when students broke rules that were enforced *occasionally.* Students comply with whatever is consistent, but they become confused and misbehave when acceptable behavior is arbitrary or not clearly outlined.

John Y. is a good example of this. John came to me because he had hit one of his classmates; he was angry and upset as he told his story. Mary had come to his desk and ripped up his paper. She had done it before, and he had told her that if she did it again, he would punch her. She did—so he did! Was that what had angered Johnny? Oh, no—you see, yesterday he hit Jimmy on the playground and his teacher only broke it up and talked to them. Today, he hits a girl and not only gets sent to the office, but Mary doesn't get anything! That was why he was angry. Whatever rules there were about fighting had not been enforced consistently.

Look around your school and mentally apply what you have said to your class, what the administrator has told the student body, and what the Student Handbook states to actual circumstances in classrooms, halls, lavatories and playgrounds. If there are inconsistencies, then you have found a trouble spot that could be a source of student behavioral problems. When you make rules that are practical, possible and positive and enforce them consistently and fairly, your school will have achieved its first major step toward reducing chronic student misconduct.

A GUIDED TOUR THROUGH A BEHAVIORAL PROBLEM

Let's visit the front lines where we work. We'll take a lad, Rodney, to show us the way. As we follow him, watch for the signposts of his development and what affects him. Many things will happen, for he is, admittedly, a composite of many students.

"I was scared the first day of school. I was late, and most of the other kids had their coats off by the time I got there. My teacher, Miss Stewart, was very nice but the kids laughed when she called me slowpoke! I got pretty red. I was so early the next day, she called me speedy, but everybody called me 'slowpoke' for a few months. First grade wasn't hard, I could read and spell and color inside the lines—but I couldn't seem to understand arithmetic.

"My school had classes where you could get help, so I was sent there by Miss Stewart. The new class was easier, but one of my friends in Miss Stewart's class said I had to be dumb to be there, and the teacher, Miss Young, treated me like I didn't know anything! I studied arithmetic hard so I could get out of there. When my parents came in for a conference, all my teachers said I was doing good. Sure enough, I went to the second grade!

"Mr. Stanton was funny. He called all the boys "little men." He took us to the playground a lot and was always fooling around with us. We had lots of stories and films in his class. The thing I remember most about him was that we almost never had homework.

"Third grade was dumb! Mrs. Watson had all the girls sit on one side and all the boys sit on the other. She was really strict. Once a week, just before we went to the playground, she read out the demerits each of us had. If we got too many, we couldn't go out. She gave them for everything. Sometimes it was months before I got to go to that playground! I was glad to get out of there because she told my parents that if I didn't get better, I was going to be in for a lot of trouble.

"She must have told Miss Hadley, 'cause the first day of fourth grade Miss Hadley told me to take a seat right up front where she could see me. She told me, right in front of everybody, that I wasn't going to give *her* any trouble because she knew how to handle boys like me. Some of the guys laughed. There were two girls in my class who got away with murder. They used to do things behind her back that my buddies and I would get blamed for. One day my friend and I decided we'd had enough, so we put some water on their chairs. Miss Hadley really got angry! They got to go home so they wouldn't catch cold, and we got detention for a week! After that, no matter what happened, we got blamed, and my marks started to go down. I was trying just as hard, but I didn't please Miss Hadley. My parents were always yelling at me 'cause I had to stay after school so much.

"That summer I decided that I wasn't going to get in trouble anymore. I told my parents, and they said that if I kept my promise I could have a dog for Christmas. School started and everything was perfect. My teacher, Mr. Miles, told us the work was going to be hard, but if we did our best we would do well. He told us the rules of our class and how he expected us to behave. When he called my name, he acted as if he had never heard of me. I worked hard and everything went well until the first week of November. We got two days off because of a big snowstorm. On the way to school after the storm, the snowballs started flying. As we crossed on to the school grounds I got clobbered, so I threw one back. One of the teachers spotted me and my friends and pulled us into the office. Throwing snowballs is a really big crime; we got office detention, and our parents were called—they were furious. The only one who seemed to understand was Mr. Miles. He said we had made a mistake and shouldn't do it again. He wrote a note to my parents, and they said they would give me another chance. I thought everything was going to be all right, but the next time the principal saw me he asked if I was staying out of trouble; then I knew he was watching me. Somehow I made it to Christmas and got my puppy. My father said that if I wasn't good, it would go to the pound. Boy, does that make me scared. It seems a long way 'til June."

Rodney's journey through four and a half years of public school education has been rocky. Can you see why? Were his teachers consistent? Were options in the school limited? Were pressures placed upon him that were too heavy? Was there enough positive reinforcement? How many Rodneys does your school produce? The behavioral problems are real, and the solutions must be equally as real.

A CASE CALLED "TOWN ELEMENTARY SCHOOL NO. 2"

In January, Rodney's father was transferred and Rodney came to Town Elementary School No. 2.

"It didn't look much different than my old school, and the books were exactly the same. Mrs. Shelly, my new teacher, reminded me a lot of Mr. Miles."

Indeed, the school was not much different from Rodney's old one. The school's population was 718 housed in a brick building built eleven years earlier. Rodney was placed on the same level as he was in his previous school. He became the thirty-first member of his class.

"I met a really nice kid named Bobby, and we got to be good friends. He has a German Shepard just like my Sandy. Mrs. Shelly lets us sit together."

"Rodney struck me as a sensitive boy, anxious to please, with good intelligence," Rodney's teacher commented. "He made a good social adjustment to his new environment and gained quick peer acceptance."

"Rodney continued learning with no change in attitude or behavior until the afternoon of February 11. During geography class a shriek went up as one of the students spotted the beginnings of snow. Eventually my class settled down, but I noticed that Rodney's behavior became more and more agitated; he appeared angry and tense. Rodney's reaction was not the glee of the others. The behavior persisted for more than an hour, and I felt compelled to request a conference."

Going to her desk, Mrs. Shelly circled a few things on a slip of paper, made several one or two word notations and called Rodney to her desk.

"Boy I knew it, here it comes again, Shelly's going to send me to the office, the office is going to call my parents, my parents are going to hit the roof, and they'll probably take my puppy away. I didn't do anything, but that won't make any difference."

"Rodney," Mrs. Shelly said, "will you take this note to Mrs. Green, please? Jane, will you show Rodney the way?" Then, turning to her class, she resumed her lesson.

Surprised, Rodney accompanied Jane down the hall. Presently, they arrived at a room where Jane introduced Rodney and he handed Mrs. Shelly's stapled note to Mrs. Green.

"I didn't know what to expect. This woman sat there, smiled, opened the note and asked me how I liked the school. We just talked for a couple of minutes, and I told her about my dog and my other school. She told me she was glad I was in the school, but she didn't know much about dogs. I don't know how we got to talking about snow, but I told her about the fight and what my Dad had said. She was cool. She told me about what this school thought and did about snowball fights. She told me how things could happen, and how I could keep from doing things that would get me in trouble. If anything happens, I'm supposed to talk to her before I do anything. She said it was nice to meet me and asked if I would like to go back to class. That was it! No hassle! I think I'm going to like it here!"

Rodney's return to class some ten minutes after Mrs.

Shelly's requested conference was smooth and did not interrupt anyone's learning. Mrs. Shelly noted that he was calmer, and at the time of dismissal was chattering away with his classmates.

Many other things happened that year in Town Elementary School No. 2, not the least of which was that on the last day of school Rodney came to Mrs. Green and showed her a picture of his dog, and his good report card.

What was it that made Town Elementary School No. 2 so different? The school was applying the Personalized Behavioral Modification Plan which opened new options and new approaches to student behavior. This school had gained a new tool. The teachers had gained another option, and the students had gained a new perspective. When it is working in a school, the Personalized Behavioral Modification Plan is a dynamic force in the educational process. The need for change is obvious. We feel that the PBM Plan, as it is explained in the following chapters of this book, insures that your school is meeting the needs of its student body. It is the way to initiate that greatly needed change.

2

Establishing the Proper School
and Classroom Environment

Knowing there is a need for change in your school is only
half the solution. A change in philosophy is the other half.

HOW TO SET THE TENOR OF YOUR SCHOOL

Traveling to so many schools, from those in very low
economic areas to places where it was not uncommon for kids
to get a twenty dollar a week allowance, I became aware that
simply by closing my eyes, I could pick up the heartbeat of
the building. Some buzz and sing, others have a rustling
stillness, others have a tenseness that is almost palpable, and a
few others are waiting to explode. I endeavored to find out
what made the difference, and what changes could be implemented to make every school come alive with education.

My discovery was fivefold: first, a consistency of rules
which we mentioned in the last chapter; second, administrators
who actively participate in the day-to-day working of their
school (let me explain: with today's curriculum conferences,
school visitations, budget problems, etc., some administrators
have become cut off from what's happening in Ms. Pease's
second-grade reading class. Yet somehow, and we do not
presume to say how, some administrators still can maintain that
day-to-day contact); third, a genuine desire to teach on the part
of most of the faculty; fourth, active, two-way communication
with parents; and fifth, a working, practical solution for
handling teachers' grievances and students' problems.

29

Whether you are a teacher or an administrator, mentally review your school and see if you can feel its pulse. If it is alive and well, rejoice. If it has a weakness, check and see if it is due to any of the above reasons. Now begins the hard work of setting the tenor of *your* school.

If it is an inconsistency of rules, use some of your faculty meeting time to set consistent rules and then religiously abide by them. If your problem is in the administration of your building, one or two unscheduled visits to two or three classrooms a week can make an astonishing difference. Don't go to observe the teacher or the class, but just to listen to a first-grader read aloud or to help a fourth-grader use an encyclopedia.

Sometimes teaching is like the fourth or fifth year of marriage: you're happy with the idea of being wed, but your mate no longer looks like a movie star. You're not unhappy, it's just that you have lost the glow of an ideal. Sometimes teachers mistake this lost idealism with a lost love of teaching, but it is not true. What is true is that the day-to-day problems are beginning to overshadow the quiet joys of an expanding child's mind. Very few teachers hear, "Gee, Ms. Jones, that was great!" as often as they hear, "That was dumb!" Keeping your mind on small successes may be difficult, but your outlook can project enthusiasm to your students.

If your problem is a misunderstanding between school and parents, open lines of communication. One of the schools I worked in was faced with the decline of PTA attendance. The teachers, sensing that it would be a problem later, formed a speaker's bureau that gave lectures to boy scout troops, Lion's Club meetings and other organizations. The one or two teachers who participated reflected back on the school, and teacher image was improved in the community.

The final difficulty is the main thrust of this book. Certainly, if teacher grievances are based on contracts and salaries, that should be handled within the local association or liaison committee. But what if the grievance concerns behavioral problems and how the building administrator is handling them? Then why not get something that will handle these problems, something whose methods and effects directly coincide with those other facets that make your school come alive? Why not set up channels of change by using the Personalized Behavioral Modification Plan?

HOW TO ESTABLISH CHANNELS OF CHANGE

When we were kids, there used to be a suggestion box in the office. Your suggestions were read by some unknown, and you probably forgot about them within a day or so. You wanted a particular teacher fired because she had kept you after school, or you wanted to abolish homework. Neither happened, but what about the suggestion you had really thought out?—the one about changing punishment procedures because they didn't seem fair, or trying to tell someone of a problem you thought needed attention. The others hadn't been acted upon and these probably wouldn't be either, so you never bothered.

Is this any different than teacher's room complaints that are never brought up at faculty meetings? Teachers complaining to other teachers and then letting the matter drop only leads to frustration and resentment when nothing is done. If, however, these problems are raised at a faculty meeting with an administrator present and receptive to suggestions, then you begin to open a channel of change. Do not use the precious faculty meeting time for things that could be better handled through administrative bulletins; rather, take the time to find solutions to problems that may have cropped up since your last meeting. Keep track of the things you wish to say. I have never seen a faculty meeting where teachers have watched the clock if something important was being discussed. Clock watchers are bored because they are not being involved.

Another channel of change is greater participation on the part of students. How is this possible? Here is an example used by a teacher to involve her class and promote understanding of how their school was run. Once a month she would set part of an afternoon aside so that her students could answer the hypothetical question, "What would you do if you ran the school?" Needless to say, some of the answers were totally impractical, but in showing why they were impractical, the students gained a new perspective on the difficulties that administrators have. She also remarked to me that occasionally one of her students would come up with a good, well-thought-out suggestion. She always tried to pass that suggestion on to the administration, or let the children themselves do it. This feeling of being actively involved in their school removed the wall that usually stood between the authority of the administration and the understanding of the student body.

Therefore, availability of the administration to the faculty and the student body, open communication within the school and the community, consistency in the classroom and school, along with efficient handling of student behavioral problems and positive reinforcement of skills and behavioral growth— these are the principles that will open your channels of change. They are also the main precepts that govern the Personalized Behavioral Modification Plan. Add confidentiality, honesty, fairness, genuine concern, humor and hard work, and you will begin to see the skeleton of the PBM Plan appear. Before going into the program itself, let's see what would happen if you applied these principles in your own classroom.

HOW TO USE PBM PRINCIPLES
FOR YOUR CLASSROOM MANAGEMENT

We are not going to deal with procedures for setting up your classroom; our main concern is what you do and say once you decide how you want to run your class. Just make certain that when you set your class rules you do not allow for situations that go against your own ideas of acceptable behavior. A case in point is a teacher who couldn't abide a student wandering around the room; yet one of his classroom rules stated that if you wanted to sharpen your pencil, you could get up and do so. The rule ran against his own personal feelings and it was a constant source of friction.

When you decide what you want your class to do and how you want them to do it, take the rules one step further and ask yourself *why* you want them to do it. If you think out each facet of classroom management logically and practically, you have built-in consistency, for you are not likely to change your personal views as easily as situations change. But, be careful of a trap: if all your statements begin with, "I want," you may be losing the rest of the major statement, namely, "What's best for the class." I knew a teacher who wanted a great deal of spontaneous classroom discussion but made a rule that students raise their hands before speaking. The reason was logical—only one person could speak at a time—but hardly practical in a situation of free-flowing ideas. The rule would better have been stated, "Raise your hand except when I suspend the rule." The teacher would still have control, and consistency of rules and attitudes could be maintained.

Another PBM principle is the efficient handling of problems arising from a disruption of your classroom management. Some teachers have good control not only over their classes, but also over themselves—others do not. To remove a student from class for a minor infraction is like shooting a mouse with an elephant gun. By removing the student, you may have lost the opportunity to show him a better way of handling the situation in the future. Chastise him? Certainly, but be sure the punishment fits the crime. Once a student was sent to me for sharpening his pencil five times within a half hour. What the child hadn't learned was the responsibility for his own actions and how to handle the new-found freedom of sharpening his pencil whenever he wanted. "You may not sharpen your pencil again until I tell you," (loss of freedom of action) would have aided the child's growth much more effectively then removal from class.

We have already seen the problems inherent in delayed punishment. As part of your classroom management, have a few ways of giving immediacy to punishment. A fourth-grade teacher I met handled minor misbehavior in a unique way: at the point of the misconduct, he told the student to look up some information in the encyclopedia pertinent to the lesson being given and present it at the end of the class period. He further stated that the student obviously didn't need any help understanding the material since he wasn't paying attention to the class. Consequently, the student was sent to do another task, was mildly rebuked in front of his peers, and usually learned that it was easier to listen in class than to misbehave and work out the material alone. One more thing, the teacher always commented favorably upon the completed assignment. "If you always did work like this," he added, "you'd be a great student, but you sometimes don't do the assignment, do you?" This method seems a practical approach to a tricky problem. The delay between misconduct and punishment is detrimental to any benefit the student might derive from the punishment. When setting your class rules be consistent, practical, fair and have an immediate punishment for most minor offenses.

Periodic discussions with your class can add to communication and understanding. Certainly, not every teacher we've met has been willing to conduct the type of discussion we mean. To them, we say that you don't know what you are missing.

My term for this is a "four-wall" discussion, meaning that anything said remains within the four walls of the classroom. Let's see how it works: the class has not been turning in homework regularly; you try everything, and nothing works. You hold a discussion. The rules are simple. You present the problem, explain your reasons for wanting homework, and then let the students talk. They might tell you they don't have to do it since they know the material already, or they can't do it because they don't understand it. Either way, your willingness to listen and your powers of persuasion will make you and your class a team working toward the solution of a common problem.

Perhaps one reason why this technique is not widely used is that some people feel that taking a student's suggestion is a sign of weakness. Yet, admitting weakness can sometimes be a great strength. I once had to take an eighth-grade math class;

my knowledge of the material was, to understate, limited. About four days into the first week I noticed that the class was restless, at times ill-mannered, and while they never actually got out of hand, I was beginning to face some difficulties. I stopped the class one day and called for a "four-wall" discussion. As I stated it, the problem was that classroom behavior was falling apart and the class was not accomplishing the work assigned. I was informed that the assignments were dumb, but I stuck to the line, "That is what was assigned." After a few mumbles, a boy in the back of the class said, "You don't know anything about math!" My first reaction, of course, was anger, but I stopped myself as the boy continued, "You do things our regular teacher does differently!" Indeed, the boy was right; the problem was now out in the open, and it needed a solution. Another student stated, "Mary is really good at this stuff. Why don't you let her explain it?" Seeing the logic in his statement, I worked out a plan whereby *I* would run the class, and *Mary and I* would handle the subject matter. The problem was solved. It can work for you, too, if you remember to take a good hold of your sense of humor before you start. Also remember that anything said during the discussion *must* be kept *strictly confidential,* for if it is not, no benefit can be derived from it.

There are, however, situations which you just cannot handle within the classroom, whether they be behavioral or academic problems. At these times you may have wished for a place where these problems could be effectively handled. May we suggest the PBM Room?

WHY THERE MUST BE A PBM ROOM

"A quiet place where students can get immediate help" —this is how the PBM Room is defined by the teachers who use it. It is an extension of the classroom's environment and procedures. It is impossible for the PBM Plan to function without a permanent base of operation. There can be very few distractions, and the atmosphere must be closed and private. An administrator told me that if I initiated the PBM in his school I could use his office. *Impossible!* First, the carryover of the administrator's authority would not help the rapport needed to pinpoint a failing student's problems in English. Second, if the administrator needed to use his office there would be no way for students to get to me, breaking the major requirement of availability within the PBM. Third, his office could not accommodate more than five people at any one time.

Probably the best reason for having a PBM Room is that it continues the learning process. The room looks much like a classroom, has an adult running it, usually has one or two kids in it, and has books, paper, desks and chairs. It is a place where students are expected to work. Now, we are calling it the PBM Room, but in practice it is called simply "Mrs. Mamchak's room." Students are quick to assign negative connotations to "special" rooms, and you don't want the PBM Plan to be negative. It is preferable that the PBM Administrator be the focal point of the students, and the PBM Plan that of the teachers and administration.

BLUEPRINT FOR THE PHYSICAL
ENVIRONMENT OF THE PBM ROOM

Look at Figure 2-1; this is a blueprint of a typical PBM Room. There are four areas, each corresponding to a factor of the Personalized Behavioral Modification Program. In some cases these divisions are real, as between punitive areas and academic aid areas, while the other divisions are imaginary. Student desks are placed in as eclectic a manner as space permits. The only mandatory placement is the Preventive Conference desk which must be placed beside the Administrator's desk and should be in the area of the room closest to the Academic Achievement Area. The setup is psychological and reinforces the principles of the PBM Plan. A student placed in the In-School Suspension Area is farthest from the Administrator's desk, while the student in the Academic Achievement Area has easy access to the Administrator. Also, note the sight lines in the area: face-to-face contact occurs in the Preventive

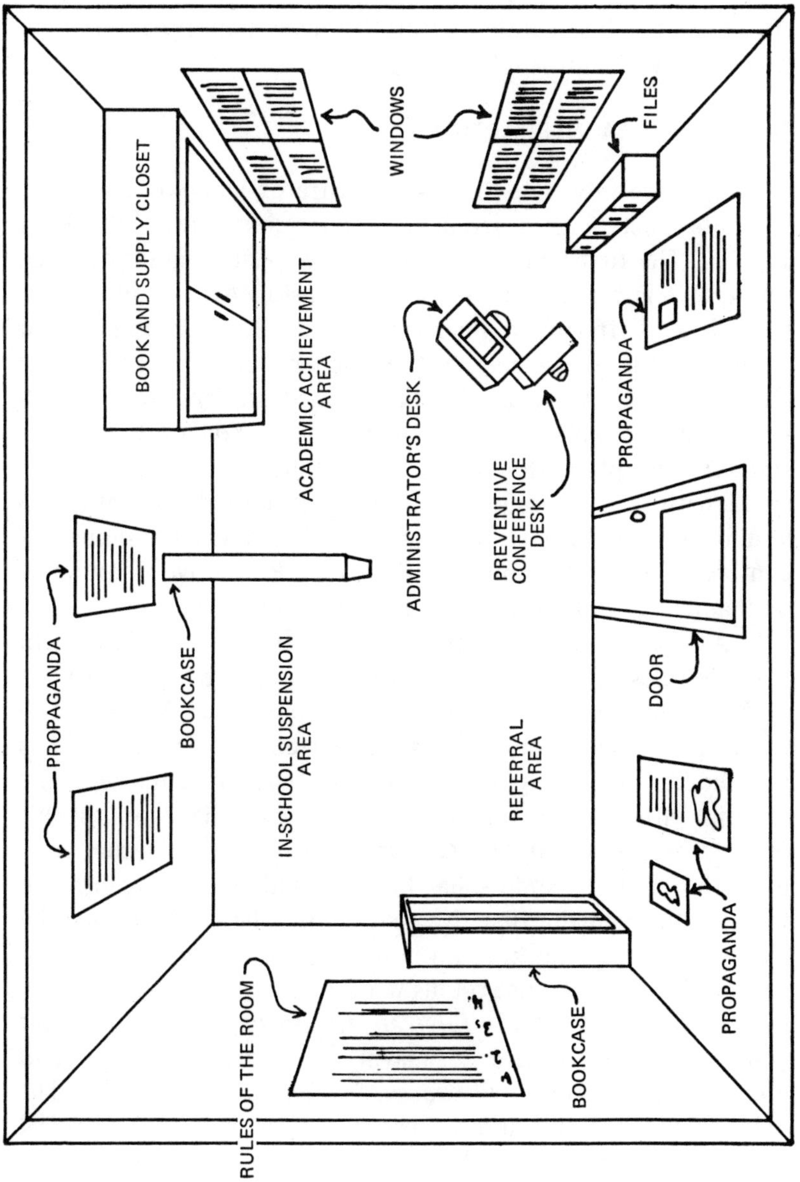

FIGURE 2-1

Labels in figure:
- BOOK AND SUPPLY CLOSET
- WINDOWS
- FILES
- ACADEMIC ACHIEVEMENT AREA
- ADMINISTRATOR'S DESK
- PREVENTIVE CONFERENCE DESK
- PROPAGANDA
- PROPAGANDA
- BOOKCASE
- IN-SCHOOL SUSPENSION AREA
- REFERRAL AREA
- DOOR
- PROPAGANDA
- RULES OF THE ROOM
- BOOKCASE

Conference, the most personal point of the program, while a visible distance is maintained at the most punitive level. Now let's see how the areas interact.

GUIDE TO AREA INTERACTION

You are now the PBM Administrator and you have four students, each with a problem that requires one of the PBM Factors. The first student has committed a suspendible offense; you direct him to the In-School Suspension Area. You walk to your desk as student number two arrives. He has been removed from class for talking back to the teacher; you direct him to the Referral Area. At that moment a third student arrives who needs time to work on a math assignment. *You walk with the student* and place him in the Academic Achievement Area, stand with him a moment until he gets started and return to you desk. Lastly, a student arrives with a teacher-requested conference form. You motion him to the Preventive Conference desk and *sit with him* to begin the conference.

As each of the first three students arrives, you have them read the rules of the room. The first one states: Keep Your Eyes on Your Own Desk. *Never* Interrupt a Conference. You verbally mention this again and go about the conference. When it is concluded, depending on what the teacher requested, the student either returns to class or stays in the room. If his problem is behavioral, the Referral Area—if academic, that area. Now the conference desk has been cleared, and you can begin working through the first three students. The student with the math problem is next; *you get up and go to him* and help if needed. If no conference on his work seems in order, you return to your desk and *call the referred student to you.* At this point you begin your conference. Having completed that you *send him* to his desk and *call the suspended student to you.* The order in which you handle these problems and your *physical movement* is important. You are there to aid students with academic problems, so they have easy accessibility to you. There is, however, an imaginary line dividing you and the students in the punitive areas. *They must come to you.* This, indeed, is how they must react to the whole program; *they* are the ones who will have to change.

Setting a second imaginary line of formality aids when working with the In-School Suspension Factor. For example, I call students by their first names in the other areas and by their surnames (John vs. Mr. Smith) in the In-School Suspension Area. The areas become definitely defined, not by placing names on them, but by your movements and actions. The students sense this, and they get the precise intention of their placement. It is now apparent that you can add innumerable students to this setup and providing there is space for them, you still can keep these areas well defined.

UNIQUE METHODS OF INFLUENCING BEHAVIOR THROUGH ENVIRONMENT

Along with the physical setup of the PBM Room, particular stress is placed on posters, mobiles and wall hangings. Each area shows positive sayings and pictures reinforcing pleasure in success. They are humorous and reach students on multiple levels of understanding. Teachers entering the room begin taking some of these ideas back to their classrooms. The more questions we are asked, the more interested we become in how the environment influences behavior.

In the 1940s propaganda buttons built anger and resolve against our nation's enemies; in the 1960s slogans built a spirit against injustice; and in the 1970s signs and posters have awakened our sense of purpose in relation to ecology. Why not take these methods and use their influence on behavioral problems?

One method which we find highly successful is using sayings from national magazines that could have a double meaning. For example, an anti-smoking slogan, "Join the unhooked generation," is coupled with an advertisement for the NEA Journal, "Use today's education to expand your horizons." The two sentences read together make a positive statement for learning. Other composites are, "Love is a beautiful way of acting tough," and "Be strong—read!" The subliminal effect of these catch phrases becomes apparent when students begin to use them and, furthermore, begin to act upon them.

A mobile is used to show that all people are needed to make the world go 'round. Cutouts of Blacks, Whites, Orientals, doctors, truck drivers, etc. are all hung from the mobile by paper clips. If someone says he doesn't like a certain nationality or occupation, you could unhook that one from the mobile, and it might teeter at a crazy angle. Put it back in the scheme of things, and the student is shown that it is necessary to keep things in balance. A simplistic example? Certainly, but it handled a second-grader's prejudice.

One last thing—sayings, buttons, and posters also can build a sense of camaraderie. Our favorite is, "Hang on Baby, June's Coming." Both teachers and students can refer to it when times get rough. Your personality can be projected in the manner that suits you best, but aim some of your media efforts at influencing behavior.

A COMMON SENSE APPROACH TO DISCIPLINE WITHIN THE PBM ROOM

There must be some order kept in the PBM Room. This is done through the posting of a short list of rules. They must be precise and easily followed and have a reason for being. Your goal is discipline, not punishment. Here is the list I work by:

1. Keep your eyes on your own desk. *Never* interrupt a conference.
2. Come prepared to work. Bring all books and materials with you. You will not be allowed to leave this room unless you have my permission.
3. Be silent. Stand and wait before you speak. Speak *only* when spoken to. Always say "please," "may I," and "thank you" when addressing me.
4. *Remember:* Always tell the truth. Make no excuses; just do better next time.

These rules are never meant for a full classroom; indeed, they are in some ways impractical and archaic. They do, however, have two strong points: first, they demand compliance without punishment. If a student does not follow the rules, he is simply ignored and cannot get what he wants. Second, they set a strict pattern of conduct with which each student is forced to comply. The student's personality, relationship to me, or reason for being there makes no difference. The rules are consistently enforced. The patterns asked for in the room are actually concentrations of socially accepted norms of behavior.

But what of the child who will not cooperate, who will not be ignored? What of the child who sings or dances or kicks over desks or is otherwise generally unbelievable? It is the philosophy of the PBM Plan that except for letting him leave the room or physically injure himself or others, there is no reaction. Let him burn himself out. When the tirade is finished, when he has exhausted himself physically and emotionally, *then* you can begin to handle him rationally. To the other students in the room, this only reinforces what you have been saying all along.

Again, let us stress the definition of discipline. It is not external, but internal. Look at the rules and you will see that students are *expected* to conduct themselves properly, not pressured into obedience by some external threat. As they comply with each rule, they learn to discipline their actions. Set your rules logically, clearly, and with socially acceptable goals in mind, and your students will begin to act accordingly. Each time they succeed will reinforce their desire to try again.

3

The Personalized Behavioral
Modification Plan--
A Four-Step Approach

The Personalized Behavioral Modification Plan is a clear, concise method of handling student behavioral problems. One of our biggest complaints with educational theories is that most teachers can't apply them in their classrooms. The theoreticians have become so far removed from the classroom that they have forgotten the little details which make those carefully planned theorems impossible to carry out. Remember when you sat in a class on Principles and Practices and heard your professor describe your prospective class of 20 bright-eyed students eager to digest every word you fed them, provided you had written beautiful lesson plans complete with behavioral objectives and motivational techniques? The reality turned out to be a class of 33, some of whom couldn't even read the textbook. Keep this in mind as we look at a practical, working plan.

A WORKING DEFINITION

The PBM Plan is a four-step procedure for handling student behavioral problems as they really exist in your school and classroom. Understanding the procedures requires a definition of terms.

The key word in the PBM Plan is "Personalized." Today, educators are using individualized testing and independent work plans in order to better suit a student's classwork to his needs and aptitude. Meanwhile, in most cases any attempt at handling behavioral problems has been through generalized rules for overall acceptable behavior. While this has posed no problem to many, perhaps even the majority of students, there are those who do not conform to the norm. Under the PBM Plan, each student's particular and individual set of problems, his "pattern" if you will, is the main focus of interest.

Behavior modification, to us, has always had the connotation of external conditioning. We try, but we can never shake the image of some poor puppy salivating as Dr. Pavlov rings his bell. Our children are not animals, and the theories using clickers, candy, time limits and punishments are deeply disturbing. Furthermore, because these techniques are external, once the external controls are removed, whatever beneficial effects were present are quickly lost. Most behavior modification programs change the environment to change the behavior. However, while special rooms, special teachers, and special situations may indeed improve behavior for the moment, what happens when the bell rings, the doors close, and they are faced with the "real" world?

Personalized Behavioral Modification is *internal*. The goal is acceptable student behavior—not just today and tomorrow, but next week and next year! Students change or modify their behavior *only* if they are shown that it is in their best interests to do so. Once misbehaving students are shown *how* to change, are given encouragement to *try* their new tools for change, and receive beneficial, *positive* reinforcement *while* they are changing, the goal is achieved. The students are the ones who are doing the "behavioral modification," not some outside monitor. Reality remains the same; the students change their perspective and learn how to deal acceptably with that reality. This basic difference in the use of behavior modification is why the PBM Plan has so much carryover.

The four steps of the PBM Plan are the Preventive Conference, the Academic Achievement Factor, Referral, and In-School Suspension. Each of these will be discussed in a chapter devoted to it alone, but a brief explanation of each seems in order.

The first factor is the Preventive Conference. In this step, we deal with potential or existing behavioral problems before they can get worse. The PBM Administrator uses the Preventive Conference to aid the students who are within the Program by setting reasonable time and work goals and by reinforcing previous discussions.

The second step is the Academic Achievement Factor. Within the PBM Plan there is a definite separation between work and behavioral problems because punishing a student who repeatedly doesn't do homework isn't helping his problem—it's just compounding it. By pinpointing weaknesses in work or study habits, the Academic Achievement Factor starts the student progressing toward success.

The Referral Factor is used when a student must be removed from class for some reason, usually disruption. The procedure for referral under the PBM Plan is much the same as it is now. The major difference is the addition of a PBM Room where the student is placed for a specified period, and where he continues to work with almost no loss of educational time.

Finally, when a student has done something which warrants exclusion from the general student body, the In-School Suspension Factor is applied. Again, the key point here is that the student is not removed from the educational process.

This, briefly, is the PBM Plan. Now let's see how it can be effective in your school.

BLUEPRINT FOR THE HOW'S AND WHY'S

Let's look at what makes a type of behavior a problem. We can almost hear you say, "I know what behavior problems are!" Indeed you do, but you are putting student's names to them, aren't you? Brian is a problem; Beth is a problem. That's not what we mean. Fighting on the playground is *your* problem; *why* Johnny hits Billy is *his* problem. Seeing this difference is difficult at times, but once seen and understood, the use of the

PBM Plan falls into place. Your students create problems for you within the framework of a classroom, but they also create problems for themselves as they struggle with their self-images. The PBM Plan reinforces goals for acceptable behavior along with providing understanding of those goals by the particular student.

You have stated, for example, that students will not lean back in chairs in your classroom. Mentally, you have completed the thought with, "Because you might fall and hurt yourselves." Ron continually leans back in his chair because he can't see the harm in it. When the PBM Administrator explains the reasoning behind the rule and gives him a *method for compliance,* the problem is solved. Do not be mislead, for not all cases are as simple as this, nor can they be so easily solved, but the reasoning is the same. Students are always given a reinforcement of *your* rules. This demands something of you; your rules must make sense.

You want a smooth-running classroom. Do it from the standpoint of *your* wants, and there will be no carryover once they have left your presence. As long as conformity is a sign of external control, this growth is not real. Set your rules along lines of socially acceptable behavior, however, and the students internalize them and the carryover, educational, and social growth appears.

There are three methods of gaining acceptable behavior: do it because I say so (power); do it because of who you are and who I am (authority); and I do it because it benefits me (discipline). Let's look at these three terms as defined in a child's home. His father has a favorite chair, and he comes home one evening to find the boy sitting in it. "Out of my chair!" booms the father, and the child scurries away. The father has exerted his *power.* Some evenings later the boy is sitting in the chair when he hears his father come in the front door. He quickly leaves the chair. In this instance the lad has accepted the *authority* of the father by saying, "That's my father's chair." Later the boy returns home with a friend. "Don't sit in that chair," he says, "It's my father's. I want to keep it for him;

he'll be home soon." The boy has achieved *discipline,* that is to say, he has internalized the order. This last step is the desire and goal of teachers when they state their classroom rules. You will note that I constantly refer to behavioral problems rather than discipline problems, for that seems a contradiction in terms. The PBM Plan's main thrust is opening paths to this third step of discipline. The reinforcement necessary for the child to understand and comply not just in the present situation but in all similar situations is what the PBM Plan gives.

A second reason the PBM Plan works is emotional distance from situations. If a student has antagonized a teacher to the point where removal is called for, both the teacher and the student are in a highly emotional state. If the emotion is anger, it is probably carried over to the administrator who places the student in the PBM Room. However, at the point where the actual punitive action is handled and positive reinforcement for future compliance is given, there is no emotional involvement.

We are amazed by the difference in the ways we handle adult's and children's emotions. When an adult is very upset, those around him try to calm him down, then find out what made him so emotional. With a child, however, we compound the problem! Speaking sharply or yelling at an upset child is like talking to any irrational human being. If control has been lost by the individual, it is imperative that it be kept by those around him. The PBM Administrator is in a position to do just this. Furthermore, this positive aid given precisely when it is most needed will be remembered. Innumerable instances of this occur when students come into my room, some itching for a fight, some sullen, some crying or loudly protesting their innocence. When they are met with a calm, interested, yet somewhat detached adult, they get control of themselves. Once that point is reached, the overwhelming beneficial consequences of the PBM Plan can come to the fore.

HOW TO SOLVE REAL PROBLEMS

Whole books could be written by teachers on the different

types of behavior they face in a normal day. No two students are alike, and no two days are exactly the same in any classroom. Looking over referral sheets, or whatever you call them in your school, you may see that there are about eight types of misconduct that most frequently lead students into trouble. Mentally check this list:

1. Classroom Distractions—frequent calling out, minor scuffles, poor attitudes, etc.
2. Assault on Persons—anything from a tussle between two students in the back of the room to a knock-down brawl on the playground.
3. Assault on Property—writing on a desk, tearing books, carving initials on doors, tearing bathroom fixtures from the walls, etc.
4. Character Violations—lying, cheating, stealing, overly shy or overly aggressive behavior. Those things in which the student involved is the most damaged.
5. Rebellion—this becomes more pronounced the older the child becomes . . . it could be anything from a first-grader saying "No!" when told to put his crayons away to a student shouting an obsenity at the principal.
6. Seasonal—snowball fights in winter and water pistol fights in June. This varies according to your part of the country.
7. Smoking—even in elementary school this has begun to be a problem.
8. Community Related—a very small fraction of behavioral problems in the school also break the community laws. This could be the possession of drugs or turning in false fire alarms.

Taking this list one more step, the teacher could make a further breakdown as to the *reasons* for these misconducts.

1. Attention Getting—the student wants the attention of his teacher, parents or some unknown person.
2. Revenge—the student wants to "get even" for some wrong, either real or imagined.
3. Peer Acceptance—to be a part of the crowd is a great motivation to most age groups.

4. Improving Self Image—for this student the danger of punishment proves his own courage and cunning.
5. Hidden Causes—no matter how much you delve into this behavior, the reason is not apparent.

No blame should be placed on a teacher for not being able to tie reasons to misconduct to discover the ideal solution for every child's problem. It is an impossible task within the framework of a classroom; yet the PBM Administrator has both the time and facilities to do it for them. We worked out a grid, explained fully in Chapter 4, which allows us to pinpoint the cause for a particular student's action, but let us give you an example now.

Mark was sent to me for talking back to his teacher. When I asked him why he was sent to me he said, "She wanted me to sit on the other side of the room 'cause I was talking." At first glance this seems a simple act of defiance. However, his next statement clarified: "She wanted me to sit next to a girl!" For Mark, a fifth-grader, the prospect of being removed from boys to be seated next to a girl would cause him to lose face. The cause of his misbehavior was peer pressure. I told him that he could have solved his problem by not talking. Having failed to do that, he could have quietly stated to his friends, "I'll be back," gone over to the assigned seat, shown a little patience, and in about 15 minutes asked the teacher if he could return to his seat, having now shown her that he could obey. When Mark returned to class, he had with him both a way of not repeating the initial offense, which was talking in class, and also a way of handling a future punitive action.

Reinforcement is given to the teacher's rule of not talking in class, and now any future situation will be viewed differently by the student. But what of problems that are continuing and not just one-time affairs?

Janie is a student in your class. It doesn't seem to matter where you place her, she is continually getting into trouble. If you take her to an assembly, you are sure she will have to be removed. You have kept her after school, contacted her parents and even sent her to the office. Nothing has been effective. Her abilities show that she easily can do the work, but she consistently gets failing marks.

Now add the PBM Plan. When Janie comes to the PBM Administrator, the only concern at the first meeting is the incident that caused the removal, not any past records. Janie is given tools to help her handle similar situations and is returned to class after a certain time. As quickly as possible, the PBM Administrator checks into her background. When Janie reports for her conference, the PBM Administrator, beginning at the point of her referral, goes over the behavior that has transpired in the last two days. The PBM Administrator mentally matches what the child is saying with what has been gathered. The distance between the student's image of herself and her actual conduct could be very wide. Having established a rapport, the PBM Administrator begins the painstaking, slow process of setting a program for Janie. Each nuance of her misbehavior must be given tools for change. Conferences are set up at short intervals to reinforce even the smallest successes. Gradually the major problems are handled. The conferences are handled at further and further intervals, and the student progresses into longer and longer periods of success. Eventually her new pattern will eliminate her need for the PBM Plan, and she will be released.

This setting of patterns is not to be misconstrued as a trip to the psychiatrist's couch. The PBM Administrator is not interested in Janie's psyche; he is interested only in getting Janie to comply with socially acceptable norms. If she has a psychological problem, the PBM Administrator's observations will be turned over to the school psychologist. The PBM Plan is not interested in the reason for actions, but in the *reasoning behind* actions. Teachers using the PBM Plan can expect primarily a change in attitude or reasoning from their students. The successes, like the problems, are tangible and can be measured.

HOW TO MEASURE SUCCESS

Certain aspects of interpersonal relationships are sensed rather than actually said or done. However, within a very short period of time tangible, measurable results can be realized from the PBM Plan.

When a student has to be removed from class, human nature dictates that you will remember the behavior when you next meet the person. What happens, however, if instead of returning to your room sullen or cowed, he enters as if nothing had happened? The change may be so subtle that you may not even be aware of it. But bring your mind back to the last time a student came back from the office. Was the re-entry into your class as smooth? Did he return to classwork as readily? Did his classmates create any stir as he re-entered?

Were there questions like, "What did they do?" or "What did you get?" Since whatever happens in the PBM Room is between the PBM Administrator and the student involved, there is no free-flowing information. The longer the PBM Plan is in your school, the deeper the sense of confidentiality, and students learn to respect it. The change becomes measurable when you realize that you haven't had to change seats so often, or you don't have the same kids staying after school all the time, or you lose that fear of being absent because of the report the substitute will leave.

I once asked a teacher how one of her students was making out. She looked at me blankly for a moment and said, "I think he's been absent, hasn't he?" Indeed, the student had been present every day but had caused so little difficulty that he had passed unnoticed. I had to laugh, but it is true. When you've been calling a student's name every five minutes because he's misbehaving, and then you don't have to for a while—he must be absent. Not at all! It's just another example of the PBM Plan helping the teacher and student get the most out of class time.

Further success is even more tangible when the Academic Achievement Factor is used. Simply, the student's grades improve in one or more subjects. Our schools are based primarily on grades; a good student gets A's and a poor student gets D's. Very seldom do we find an A student who is a behavioral problem or a D student who is an angel. As behavior more nearly approaches a norm, so do grades. As grades get better, so does behavior. Again, do not fall into the confusion that the PBM Plan is going to help a student with borderline handicaps. A perceptually impaired child will not become a perfect reader through the PBM Plan any more than a hyperactive child will become a placid student. What the PBM Plan *will* do is solve behavioral problems so that normal aptitudes and abilities can produce better grades and performance.

CHECKLIST FOR YOUR CLASS

Picture your classroom. Take your time—remember each child's face, actions and even your own outlook toward them. As you go over your classroom, pick out the problems and the previous ways you have handled them. There will probably be three or four students to whom your mental eye continuously returns. Put these names aside for a moment, for they are your problems and we are going to seek solutions.

Along with their names, add what you think are their problems: they don't like school, they are lazy, they're dumb—be subjective, say what you wish; no one but you will see this information.

If you are wondering why we are having you do this, let us postulate that one of the reasons that some children as well as adults don't like school is because the teacher is the first person they met who didn't love them and who didn't think that everything they did was wonderful and cute. It may sound silly, but it could influence a child's work in school or an adult's vote on the school budget.

Now, look at the list you just made. Are you doing anything to foster this belief? Teachers, too, can fall into simplistic traps. A common one is the blond-blue-eyed-bright dark-dirty-dumb syndrome. Some students strike us as being perfect while others, for some unknown reason, repel us. Before you close this book and say that we are on a "prejudice" soapbox, remember that we said we were going to be realistic and practical. Glance at your list of names and see if there is any common denominator *besides* behavior. If there is, rethink your values. If there isn't, then the PBM Plan can help you.

HOW TO "PLUG IN" TO EACH FACTOR

Even though the PBM Plan is composed of four coordinated steps, each factor can be dealt with separately. Once you have gone over the checklist for your class, let us imagine that one of the problems is work-oriented while the others are behavior-oriented. The Academic Achievement Factor is so designed that a student does not have to be in behavioral difficulties to be placed in it.

Take your problem child. Do you know what his basic problem is? Is it lack of homework, poor test scores, or incomplete or incorrectly done class work? You may not be able to pinpoint it exactly, but there must be some observable behavior, or you wouldn't consider it a problem. A short note to the PBM Administrator alerts her to the child and the facts you have observed. At that point the PBM Administrator begins setting up a program toward academic success for that child in your classroom.

Your observations are necessary as a starting point. Once you have spotted the problem, whether work or behavioral, the PBM Plan stands ready to go into operation. If your list includes behavioral problems, your observations are vital: something in the behavior has signaled trouble. When you inform the PBM Administrator of this, your helpful background information will set the program.

The next two steps of the PBM Plan, Referral and In-School Suspension, are suggestions made by you. The PBM Plan will work closely with you toward the goal of the student's re-entry into your class.

And finally, the Preventive Conference is your major plug

into the PBM Plan. Teacher input is most effective in this step. We've always hated long, involved forms which usually have to be made out in triplicate and are time consuming. Therefore, the form for a teacher-requested conference is a simple checklist. (See Chapter 12.)

Conversations between teachers are another source of information. You can alert the PBM Plan to a potential problem even if it has not directly affected you. An example of this is a conference called for by an eighth-grade science teacher. He was talking to a fellow faculty member about one of the students already in the Program. It seems that the boy had made a new friend who seemed to be leading him back into old habits. The teacher told the PBM Administrator about the new friend because he feared some backsliding on his student's part. The friend also got into some trouble, but his teacher had not referred him to the PBM Plan. The science teacher's analysis of the problem was correct. A Preventive Conference was held with the boy in the Program to give him encouragement to continue his success, and the friend was also checked to see if the PBM Plan could be of assistance to his teacher. The outcome was that the boy did not slip into old problems and patterns, and the friend's conduct was also changed. The potential trouble spot was settled before it ever caused either one difficulty.

Particular stress should be placed on the commodity of time. Your classroom time is precious; the PBM Plan conserves your time in the classroom. You will be freer to pursue classroom interactions and your time and the students' time will be more productive. When you plug in your students to the PBM Plan, the five or ten minutes needed for a conference will save you hours of educational time. Student problems are handled quickly, efficiently and successfully.

The student benefits, and so do you!

4

An Inside Look at a Preventive Conference

The Preventive Conference Factor of the PBM Plan is basic; if *it* is not successful, the Program cannot succeed. It is at this point of personal contact that *Personalized* Behavioral Modification begins.

HOW TO ESTABLISH RAPPORT WITH THE INDIVIDUAL STUDENT

Each of us speaks in a manner conducive to understanding. Most of us can do this easily with our peers, but speaking to people much younger or much older than ourselves is sometimes difficult. Even if we have trained ourselves to speak to one age group (for example, the first-grade teacher speaking to her class), it may still be difficult to speak as easily to another age group. The PBM Administrator, however, must be understood by all.

Establishing rapport calls for some seemingly unrelated factors. The PBM Administrator may be called upon to draw from a wide range of outside activities in order to reach a student. For example, at one time I raced cars, and when one of my students was having trouble communicating with me, I asked him why he wanted to stay in school. His answer of "I want to take Driver's Ed. in high school!" showed his interest in automobiles. Coupling my knowledge with his interest, I established a rapport, which was then used to spur his interest in reading (I got him some automobile manuals) and eventually to

54

improve his whole academic outlook. Another teacher I know was quite good in art and could easily establish rapport using her artistic abilities. Use your expertise!

The fact that you know or can do something that is of great interest to the student is an asset that cannot be overly stressed. It is tangible proof that you understand *their* world. The interest thus generated gives credence to the suggestions you make on how they can change their behavior. If you cannot relate to the problems that a boy-crazy seventh-grade girl can encounter, it may be difficult to give her the precise tools that she will need to handle the situation.

Want a suggestion? If your ear can stand it, listen to the local popular-music station for at least a half hour every day. It is amazing the amount of slang you will pick up. Start glancing through sports sections of newspapers. Knowledge of the standings of personalities involved in major league sports can be of great help to you. At least once a month check the front pages or covers of magazines with which your students might come in contact (*Mad, Photoplay, Disc*); it might give you clues to what they are reading. Finally, try to keep abreast of the things that are going on in your school. If a new book has been introduced in the second grade or one of the classes is preparing for a play, the fact that you know about it shows an overall interest on your part in what is happening and also a point of reference if the student mentions it.

Being a PBM Administrator is a full-time job. What you read, hear or see today may provide the key for helping a troubled student tomorrow.

HOW TO PINPOINT THE PROBLEM

At each step of the PBM Plan there is a Preventive Conference. It is imperative that you pinpoint the problem and the reasoning behind the student's behavior as quickly as possible. We found that by asking certain questions in a precise order, the reasonings became apparent. The longer we worked at it, the more the responses fell into categories, with each category showing something different and also giving us a clue on how to handle the student's difficulty. Once having established the reasoning, we could then provide them with tools for handling their particular problems. Remember, the quicker you find out what the student's problem is and the sooner you can give him the tools for change, the quicker you can show the achievement of success.

We based Preventive Conference interviews on three questions:

1. What did you do to be sent here?
2. Why are you here?
3. Since I wasn't there, describe to me what happened.

When you have the answers to these questions, you have three points of reference. The answer to the first shows you how the child views the incident that led him to the room; the answer to the second question shows his understanding of his own actions; and finally, within the description lie the possible reasons for the behavior.

No matter at what point the student enters the PBM Plan, the Preventive Conference is always the first step. In the beginning, almost all Preventive Conferences come from Referrals or In-School Suspensions. Eventually, Preventive Conferences will be used for Academic Achievement and finally used as a factor for student aid. Let us see how the answers to three questions can form the program for the PBM student.

Look at the first column in Figure 4-1. The answers to the first question, "What did you do to be sent here?" fall into five categories:

1. Denial
2. Acceptance
3. Self-Accusatory
4. Peer-Accusatory
5. Authority-Accusatory

There are also about five possible answers to the question "Why are you here?" that further help place it into one of the categories. With the final question, "Describe what happened" there are 20 to 25 possible answers which can be placed into categories that show where the child is in his thinking at this point and in this particular incident. It is not a pattern until he fits it more than once.

What did you do to be sent here? Why are you here?	I wasn't there. Describe what happened.			
DENIAL	FRAMED	PEER LIED	AUTHORITY LIED	TOTAL NON-ACCEPTANCE
"Nut'in!"	"I don't know . . . "	"Tommy said . . . but I didn't!"	"Mr. X told my teacher . . . but it wasn't true!"	"I didn't do nothing — and even if I did, what's wrong?"
ACCEPTANCE	IDEAL	PEER TURNED IN (so it's OK)	AUTHORITY ORIENTED (so it's OK)	DEFEATED
"I did . . ."	"I did something wrong."	"I did . . . Timmy told the teacher I was wrong and . . ."	"Mr. X told us we'd get in trouble, I did . . ."	"I did . . . you can do anything you want because I was wrong."
SELF-ACCUSATORY	IDEAL	PEER (made me do it)	AUTHORITY	POOR SELF-IMAGE
"I did a bad thing!"	"I don't know why."	"Jim told me to . . . then I got in trouble."	"The teacher told me to . . .	"I can't do anything right!"
PEER-ACCUSATORY	FRAME	PEER REJECTION	PEER ACCEPTANCE	PEER DIS-ORIENTATION
"Billy did . . ."	"I got caught, but he didn't!"	"Billy doesn't like me!"	"We all thought it was fun . . ."	"I don't like . . ." "They all hate me!"
AUTHORITY ACCUSATORY	TEACHER	ADMINISTRA-TION	HOME	SOCIAL UNDEFINED
"The teacher said I did . . ."	"Mrs. X doesn't like me!"	"The Principal doesn't like/ wouldn't believe me!"	"My parents told me . . ." My parents don't care!"	"They always say . . ."

FIGURE 4-1

Let us take you back to Chapter 2 for a moment. Remember how we defined six categories of reasonings for student misconduct? Now having worked the grid with the student, you may note that the particular misbehavior in any particular incident may be easily pinpointed in terms of one of these reasons.

Let's take an example: Judy is sent to you by her teacher for "general disruption of class!" Judy enters the room and is motioned to the Preventive Conference desk. You glance at the referral sheet, then look at Judy and ask, "Judy, what did you do to be sent here?" "Miss Jones threw me out," says Judy. "Yes, I know that, but why are *you* here?" "Well, Melissa wrote on my desk so I took my crayon and scribbled on her paper, and Miss Jones threw me out!"

If you apply Judy's answers at this point to the grid in Figure 4-1, you have narrowed it down to two of the five categories, Peer-Accusatory or Authority-Accusatory. Now let's carry it one step further.

"I wasn't there, Judy, so suppose you just tell me in your own words what happened." Judy shuffles in her seat and begins, "Melissa is always telling lies about me, and she tells the other kids not to sit with me when we have lunch. She's always doing mean things." "Yes, Judy," you interrupt, "But what happened today?" "She wrote on my desk, and the kids started to laugh. That's when I took my crayons and did it!"

Viewing the grid, we can now see that her outlook is Peer Accusatory, and her problem lies in Peer Rejection. Study the grid; can you see how we have arrived at this? Now going back to Chapter 2, we can place Judy's problems under the *reasoning* of Peer Acceptance.

Now that you have pinpointed the problem, Judy's lack of peer acceptance, you must give her a tool by which she can handle her difficulties with Melissa and still not lose ground with her peers. For example, to tell this student to rely on the teacher and report Melissa's future misconduct would be the gravest mistake, for it would completely alienate her peers, compounding the problem. When Melissa does something wrong, wouldn't it be better for Judy to say, as loudly as possible, "Melissa, that is the dumbest and most childish thing I have ever seen!" and laugh at her? Unbeknownst to Judy, you then inform her teacher of the problem and the suggested solution and put Judy on a Preventive Conference schedule.

If you think that this example is too simple, consider that except for the alterations necessary for secrecy, this actually occurred. The student we call "Judy" resolved her problems and at the same time, "Melissa" learned some very valuable lessons in living.

WHY THERE MUST BE CONSISTENCY, HONESTY, AVAILABILITY AND CONFIDENTIALITY

The role of consistency in the PBM Plan cannot be overstressed. Whenever a child sees you, whatever your personal feelings and regardless of the circumstances surrounding the conference, your attitude and manner must be the same. "How can I best help this child use his full potential?"—these should be your watchwords and should be ever present in your mind. That is your reason for being there, not chastisement or punishment. Once you have started the Preventive Conference schedule, you must commit yourself to working with that student until the obstacles are overcome. For some, this will be fairly easy and may be accomplished in perhaps two weeks. For others, it may be a long procedure lasting several months. My favorite phrase with these latter students is, "I'll turn you every way but loose!" Indeed, the very fact that you are consistent with the difficult cases builds the reliability and success of the Program.

You may wonder why we stress honesty, but how can two individuals communicate without it? The honesty to which we are referring begins with the administrators and finds its fruition in the students. After all, from the time we were very small, lying has served us well. It got us out of trouble, prevented anger, shifted blame or saved someone's feelings. It has many advantages. The PBM Administrator takes the advantage out of lying. The trouble will be handled; there is no anger displayed; no blame is ever mentioned; and no one's feelings have to be saved, certainly not the administrator's, and with the strict use of confidentiality, no one else knows what is said. Honesty not only becomes the best policy, but the only policy. In the two years I have worked with the program, only four students ever lied to me. My kids were not paragons of virtue; there was simply no advantage in it.

We've stated the need for a PBM Room: the reason is availability. Let us analyze your thinking for a moment. If we say "the office," don't you think of a place? The same holds true for the PBM. When a student is in need of a conference, there has got to be a place to go. Carrying the analogy one step further, when the building administrator is not in the office, word is left on how to contact him. Again, the PBM Administrator must be easily located when not in the room. This may be done in many ways; I use signs posted on my door. Usually, the need to see the PBM Administrator is immediate. Never put off a student arriving for a conference; that is basically why you are in the school. You must be available when you are needed.

Finally, imagine what would have happened in our last example if Melissa had found out that Judy was talking about her? Nothing would have been gained, and a great deal would have been lost. When you are speaking with a student in a Preventive Conference, the atmosphere must be closed, that is to say, private between you and the student. Since the tools for change are designed just for *that* student, your information is personal. Even when you abstract the problem for the teacher, you must never repeat what the student has said. A sense of fairness and propriety prevents telling secrets between adults, and secrecy is even more important with children.

Consistency, honesty, availability and confidentiality are your tools for helping students handle their problems.

PROVIDING THE TOOLS AND INCENTIVE FOR CHANGE

Let's get down to basics. How do kids change? What are these "tools" that we are talking about? What incentives? Every teacher has that "bag of tricks" we mentioned before, but those are geared to a class. The tools the PBM Administrator offers are for one student in a particular set of circumstances. The list is endless, and there is no way to tell you precise methods. For clarity, we will give you a few examples, but keep in mind that every PBM Administrator has to devise the specifics himself. I gave the following tools my own nicknames, but use whatever ones you like.

1. *The Actor*

This is the tool given to the student that changes his behavior while making him feel that he is putting something over on his teacher.

Bobby was having trouble in Mr. Griffith's class. He called out, did not raise his hand, and had been removed for disrupting class several times. "Look, Bobby," I finally said, "Let's do a number on Mr. G. for a couple of days. Why don't you raise your hand, stay in your seat and do all the other things he seems to want. Then if he throws you out we'll look at the problem in terms of him. But remember, Bobby, for it to work, you have to do what he says." Bobby had a tool for sociably acceptable behavior that he thought was a weapon against his teacher. He went back to class, wielded his new weapon, and at the follow-up conference several days later stated, "Boy did I put one over on him! He couldn't throw me out! I'm gonna try that in all my other classes and see if it works there, too!"

2. *Gotcha!*

This is a tool given for use by one student to defend himself from another. The situation usually runs like this: student X does something to student Y, who retaliates and gets caught while student X gets off without punishment. The tool changes the situation this way: student X does something to student Y (now in the Program), who instead of retaliating, says loud enough for the teacher to hear, "X, why did you do . . . " The result is that the teacher would investigate the outburst, and X would be caught. Y does not get in trouble!

3. Hooray For Me!

This particular tool is used for the academically oriented problem. Somewhat similar to *The Actor,* it has the student working seemingly against the teacher.

Rosie was sure she was going to fail spelling because she felt that the teacher thought she was dumb. She had an English assignment due in the next couple days. After her work was finished in spelling, I said to her, "Have you started that English assignment?" "No," she answered. "O.K., let's work on your spelling teacher. In your English assignment let's see how many of your spelling words you can use. When you finish it, make sure it is all spelled right. Then, why don't you ask your spelling teacher to look it over for *grammar,* telling her that you are working for a good mark in English. Don't even mention the spelling words—see if she notices." Nine times out of ten, the teacher remarks about the good spelling of the poor spelling student.

The list goes on. With the variations, there is one to fit almost every situation. Please note that the result of each one of these "tools" is a student exerting effort for socially acceptable behavior and academic success. The incentive is success, and the tools work. They do precisely what the student thinks they are going to do. Regardless of the reasons used in the beginning, the student succeeds, and success becomes habit forming. And that's what you want—you want them hooked on success! It doesn't matter why Bobby behaved in Mr. Griffith's class; conforming to the rules brought him success, and he will do it again! Extra effort earned Rosie a pat on the head. She will work twice as hard to get the next one!

Make the tools work, and let the success happen. Reinforce the student's role in his own behavior, and believe me, new patterns will form!

HOW TO KNOW WHEN TO CHANGE STRATEGY

A Preventive Conference schedule which is properly geared

runs a definite course. In many ways it is like a stay in the hospital. There is intensive care, followed by operative, post-operative, convalescent and release. As with some deep-seated illnesses, more than one operation may be needed. Continuing our analogy, as there are different medications at different times, so there are different strategies at different times in a Preventive Conference schedule. In the beginning, the tools must be such that they bring immediate success. This is not the time to plan long-range goals. Each tool is to be used for a specific incident and for handling a specific problem. Once the student begins to show signs of being able to handle these immediate problems, you slowly begin to shift emphasis to somewhat longer terms. You might have to work on every night's homework in the beginning and then switch to weekly assignments. At the point where the student can handle this intermediate stage, you might easily extend him a little further. If the stretch isn't too far, then you can switch into long-range goals (for example, the end of the marking period). When to start each of these steps is shown to you by the student's progress. If the student is getting into difficulty every two or three days, then see him every two days; if he can handle himself for a week—once a week. Never extend the conference schedule further than is realistic for the student's success. Each student works at his own pace, and you must keep the success factor going. To release a student prematurely is a failure on the part of the PBM Administrator in judging the growth of the student.

AN EXAMPLE OF A PREVENTIVE CONFERENCE

Because each Preventive Conference is different, selecting one from the hundreds that I held is an almost impossible task. Instead, let's take one student and show his entire schedule of Preventive Conferences.

Charles was referred to me during his first period math class. The series of questions brought the following: "I was running around the room. I was chasing Jim and running around

Mr. Simpson's class." Since it was the first time I had seen Charles, and he had freely admitted that he did something wrong, I gave him the simple suggestion of staying in his seat, had him complete the work given, and in approximately an hour, had him returned to class. I also scheduled him for a conference the following Wednesday, thus giving myself enough time to check with his teachers. I discovered that Charles was an average student with normal ability and good peer acceptance. He was, however, characterized by one of his teachers as being easily led. In situations where control from the teacher was relaxed, Charles tended to get into difficulties.

The conference on Wednesday began with my question, "How is it going?" "Not too bad," he answered, "but I'm failing math, and the teacher is really giving me a hassle." This answer caused me to direct that conference to this second problem. I told him to check in with me on Friday, and we would look into how he was handling his homework. Since he had been removed from math class and seemed to be failing math, and the fact that the math teacher ran a very loose class, the direction that Charles needed was pinpointed. His two-day tool was to do his homework *and* to observe his teacher's reaction to *other* students' behavior. He was not to participate in any further misconduct.

Friday's conference was very brief. He had done his homework and stayed out of difficulty. The tool of observing had been successful, and he told me that Mr. Simpson seemed to let the kids do what they wanted as long as they did not interfere with class. I stated that if that was the case, perhaps it would be better if he didn't interfere with the class. Since he hadn't solved his problem in math, I arranged another conference for a week later. Behaviorally, he had survived the week and had done all of his homework except for the day before. Obviously, a week was as far as he could go at this point.

Charles had weekly conferences for one month. There were no incidents of misconduct for about six weeks, when he again got in trouble in Mr. Simpson's class. This time, however, Charles was sent on a teacher-requested conference rather than a referral. Reinforcing the past two months of success, Charles was able to bring his actions into line, and almost three months to the day of his first referral I received the following note from Charles's teacher:

> "Charles is not an outstanding student, but his work has shown a marked improvement in neatness and accuracy. His behavior is tremendously improved. He listens carefully, follows directions and obviously tries to maintain his self-control."

Charles had made his own adjustments and was now performing in a socially acceptable manner. With one final conference to let him know that he could come back whenever *he* thought *he* might need it, I released him.

This Preventive Conference schedule used the grid, tools for change, a change in strategy, and the building of a pattern of success. It achieved its purpose: it worked!

5

Dynamics of the Academic
Achievement Factor

Since there is a definite separation within PBM of work and punishment, the Academic Achievement Factor is a vital step in the educational growth of the students. The failing student who is frustrated and feels defeated begins a slow spiral downward. The Academic Achievement Factor is always geared *upward,* toward success.

A TEACHER'S GUIDE TO THE USE OF THE
ACADEMIC ACHIEVEMENT FACTOR

Call them poor students, under-achievers, or slow learners, there are those in your class who don't keep up. The symptoms may vary from no homework and poor test scores to procrastination and missed assignments. Understand, we are not dealing here with easily recognizable learning disabilities. Most teachers have unbounded patience with the student whose abilities prevent optimum performance. Friction arises when a student of *good* ability does not perform up to capacity. If Phil does not turn in his homework for two weeks, there is liable to be an explosion, yet this explosion may not produce more homework; in fact, it may produce even less. With the AAF, teachers are given a new way of handling this very basic work problem.

In the beginning of the year, all students start out equally. Within two weeks, however, most classes start falling into that infamous bell-shaped curve. Some of the students are joys to behold, while some lack the skills to comply with even the simplest homework assignments. In the middle, however, rests the majority of your class; this is where the basic teaching is done. There are many methods which teachers use to inspire these average students. If the student is exerting effort, there is no problem. If, however, he is "goofing off," something must be done.

Within the Academic Achievement Factor of the PBM Plan:

1. When homework is not forthcoming, the student is placed on a work schedule.
2. For poor test scores, teachers request a work period.
3. For incomplete assignments, a work period.
4. For procrastination, a work schedule.

Let us see how the teacher benefits from this.

Turning in homework produces significant changes in performance. When a student understands what is going on in class, he will participate. The more he participates, the more he gets out of a class. The more he gets out of a class, the better his grades become. These causative factors are the reasons for homework, and the PBM Plan reinforces them.

Not properly studying for a test can cause a poor test score which the actual understanding of the material does not warrant. We find that some students do not test well because they do not have good study habits. Assistance to the student at the precise time when he must concentrate his efforts shows remarkable results. I see a student the day before a test (I do not know what is on it) to have him pick out what he thought would be on the exam. When I see him the day after with his smile and passing score, it causes me to believe that *this* step of the PBM makes the rest of it worthwhile. When a teacher notices that a student is slipping, the call to the Academic Achievement Factor can bring the success they both seek.

HOW TO SEPARATE WORK AND PUNISHMENT

We never actually sat down and graphed the relationship

between behavioral problems and poor work, but it certainly can be noted that a student's frustration in his school work has side effects such as inattentiveness in class, disruption and other behavioral difficulties. Trying to handle too many changes at once is confusing for some of the students I face; for some, indeed, behavior is their biggest problem. In these cases I handle this first. But for others, the need to succeed in the traditional sense for their parents or relatives, means better grades. For these students, success in academics leads to social changes. When a student is sent to me for Academic Referral there are usually comments on the teacher's notes like, "Nice kid, but lazy—Smart, no homework—Great one-on-one, but I can't get him to work in class." These statements indicate a need to reinforce good study habits and to develop a pattern of academic success.

To punish any of these students under present options is to associate academic problems with social misconduct. This link just isn't true. Our society does not care if Billy gets 100% on his English test; it is more concerned if he breaks a window.

Teachers become aware that some problems are work-oriented and send students for a work period. During this period, the student works on the same material he would have in class but in a quieter, calmer atmosphere. This is not to say that the child is coddled, but rather that class work is reinforced exactly to the student's needs.

For the student who performs one-on-one but not in class, specific emphasis is placed on why he becomes distracted in class. As clearly as you can pinpoint a behavioral problem, you can pinpoint an academic one.

HOW TO ANALYZE THE STUDENT'S PRESENT WORK PATTERN

As there is a grid for behavioral problems (Chapter 4, Figure 4-1), there are also divisions for academic problems. When asked, "What do you think your problem is?" students replied:

1. "I don't understand . . . "
2. "Last year we did . . . , this year it's different."
3. "The teacher has us do too much . . . "
4. "I like (subject), but I don't like (subject)."
5. "I don't get assignments in on time because . . . " (social reason)
6. "I don't do the assignments because . . . " (academic reason)
7. "I didn't do the work because . . . " (physical reason)

Starting with the student's analysis, the Academic Achievement Factor begins to analyze what caused his Academic Referral. Again, let us emphasize that this search is without *condemnation*. The first step is not to rebuke, but to find out *why*. The PBM Administrator's role in this first step is that of a detective. The "missing person" for whom the PBM Administrator and the student are searching is the academically successful student. To aid in the search I have the student keep a diary for *two* days. The specific things he is to write in his diary are when he studies, what he does when he is given a homework assignment, what he does in class when given free time, and some of the activities he participates in at home. It is not to be long. Sometimes the solutions become so obvious that the child comes in after two days and says something like, "I watch too much television!"

The second step in the detective work is done by the PBM Administrator and the student's teachers. What kind of assignments does the student do (he does creative writing but does not do exercises; does drawings but will not write essays; etc.)? Is there any continued success in any subject? With these pieces of the puzzle, the PBM Administrator draws up a short analysis of the student's present work pattern. I always notify the parents at this point to enlist their aid. These conversations sometimes provide additional clues to the patterns. By the time the student arrives for a conference, I have an analysis that might look something like this:

"Andy is doing poorly in math and science. He performs very well in class but does very little homework; he will do a couple examples in math, but never all. In English and social studies he makes a great effort to research little known facts and report his knowledge to the teacher. He is a poor speller. He is a Little League ball player, a newspaper carrier, and he swims at the local YMCA. He has a group of friends who play together."

With this analysis and the student's diary, the PBM Administrator is now ready for the second step in identifying the weakness.

CHECKLIST FOR IDENTIFYING PRECISE AREAS OF WEAKNESS

Because the impetus for change is on the student, the PBM Plan *and* the student must identify the areas of weakness. The whole idea is to have the student discover what he is doing, give him ways to overcome the weakness, and let him act upon them and take credit for his own success. With the student's diary and your analysis at hand, watch out for areas that can produce difficulties. Of all the students in the AAF, in our experience better than 85% fit one or more of these categories:

1. Does not go home directly after school.
2. Does not take home books in which he has assignments.
3. Does not have a set time to be in the house after dinner.
4. Has unlimited play time regardless of the amount of homework.
5. Has no set place to study.
6. Has unlimited time to watch TV regardless of homework.
7. Has more than 40% of out-of-school time taken up with family chores and social responsibilities.
8. Does not write down future assignments.
9. Usually does not tell his parents what he has for homework.
10. Does not stay for extra help.
11. Does not have a set way to bring homework to school from home.
12. Does not study for tests.
13. In order to avoid trouble, will copy from another student.
14. Does not turn in legible homework.

15. Does not finish work started in class at home or does not start work at all.
16. Does not bring to school required materials for class projects.

As each of these difficulties is stated, you can see that its converse would be a solution. For example, if he doesn't go home directly after school, then tell him to go home directly! If you are looking for simple answers, however, this is not the way to do it! His returning home directly from school may be a causative factor, but not the main problem. As a detective can never jump to conclusions without all the facts, so must the PBM Administrator have *all* the information before setting a program.

Another factor that should not be overlooked is what is *not* said in conjunction with what *is* said. This is particularly true when talking to parents. If, when you ask about their child, they make no mention of set dinner times, play habits or chores, these ties to the family may not exist. If, indeed, the child's home life and school life do not mutually reinforce each other, you may have found the key to the student's problem. Do not be afraid to take as much time as needed before setting a plan for the student's success. The more time you take to make it precise, the greater the success and the growth of the student's self-confidence. Once started, the program must gain momentum. Therefore, make certain you have everything you need before you begin.

GUIDELINES FOR BUILDING A PATTERN OF SUCCESS

Having acquired the proper picture of the student's academic problems, you now begin a five-step program:

1. Find the easiest solvable factor.
2. Suggest the simplest and most easily performed solution.
3. Set the shortest, yet most practical, time span for performance.
4. As soon as indications of success are shown, reinforce the progress.
5. Building on past success, start with the next factor.

These five steps have a built-in insurance of success which you must have in the beginning. Let's say that Billy has 12 out of the 16 difficulties, but the easiest problem to solve is that he does not take his books home. We're not interested in whether he does his homework at first, but just that he takes his books home. If he takes them home for one week, for Billy this is an accomplishment. A simple statement such as, "See, if you put your mind to it, you *can* remember to take your books home," is all the reinforcement he needs for this particular facet of the problem. Now you can go on to another facet which may be harder to solve. In the meantime, you have already implanted in Billy's mind the thought, "If I could do that, maybe I can do this!" Working from the simplest to the hardest can be a painstaking process, but the end result is an academically oriented student.

When the program is first started, the PBM Administrator's role is very directive. *You* are providing the solutions, and the student is acting upon *your* suggestions. The more you delve into the more difficult problems, however, the less directive your role must become. You are building the *student's* self-confidence. To insure the growth of this self-confidence, the *student* must begin to find his own solutions.

SUPPORTIVE MEASURES FOR INSURING
A CONTINUATION OF ACADEMIC ACHIEVEMENT

The key to the whole process is positive reinforcement. We're sure you realize how important a single statement of praise can be when given to a child who is trying his hardest. We divide the supportive measures into two categories, home and school. Parents who remark approvingly and show awareness of their child's attempts increase the child's willingness to continue in order to gain more approval. I constantly remind parents to be aware of the changes in attitude and productivity in their children. Even if the end result of all the student's efforts is still a D, but he has done something to show he was trying, I ask them to stress *this* rather than the D. Eventually the grades will come up, but long before the grades will come an improved self-image.

The other side is the school. As a teacher gathers in last night's homework and finds a usually nonproductive student's work, how immensely important is a statement of *genuine* approval, "Why, John, you did your homework." Be careful— any indication of sarcasm or belittling will destroy his reason for working and his efforts to change.

Even if there are small slips in the child's progress, and there may well be, always accent the successes already achieved. Some problems are harder to solve than others, but remember that patience, understanding and reinforcement make all goals attainable.

The Academic Achievement Factor may best be summed up as a massive, directive, positive dose of distilled education. It is not that other students get less in a normal classroom situation, but the students within the PBM Plan need more. To show how this educational tool is actually applied, let's take a look at one of my students whom we will call "Mike."

A BOY NAMED MIKE

Mike is a seventh-grade boy who got into some behavioral difficulties in the sixth grade but had not been referred to the PBM. The first indication of trouble came when Mike was referred to me on November 16. He was not a behavioral problem but was sent because he had not started a rather lengthy science project that had been given two weeks before and was due the next day. With him came the dates of the assignment and a rather furious note from his science teacher. There were no actual indications of what the teacher specifically wanted me to do except to get Mike to do this project. Obviously, Mike's problem went much deeper than any single assignment, so I sent the teacher a note stating that I would put Mike on a work schedule, and that since the marking period would be ending in three days I suggested that Mike be given the failure which he deserved for this marking period, and the main thrust of the Academic Achievement Factor be toward next marking period. To this the teacher agreed. Within fifteen minutes I had this information and began to work with Mike.

Starting with the science assignment, I asked why he had not completed his work. "I didn't know I was supposed to do it! I didn't understand the assignment!" A string of excuses placing the blame in a buckshot fashion followed. It was everybody's fault but his. In a somewhat light manner I asked if he thought *he* had anything to do with the assignment at all. Rather sheepishly he replied, "Well, maybe . . . " "What do you think you could have done?" He started to say he could have done the assignment but immediately sidetracked himself by saying that it wouldn't have mattered anyway because he didn't understand it. My first impression analysis was poor self-discipline coupled with a low self-image.

The first task that I set for Mike was to keep the two-day diary. Mike agreed, and I said I would see him in two days. He asked about his science project, and I told him he would receive an F. I further told him that this failure belonged in this marking period, but that we would be concentrating on the future. Mike's reaction was halfhearted.

I did not get to Mike's teachers until the next morning. The information I gathered at that time was that Mike would fail eight out of his nine subjects. He was characterized as lazy, inattentive, poor in attitude, displaying minor misconduct and uncooperative. The only positive note I heard was from the teacher of his only passing subject, civics. Mike seemed to enjoy and always did well in this subject, even to the point of doing research and extra reports. Somehow, this picture of Mike going through encyclopedias and making several trips on his own to the library seemed quite incongruous. No explanation was given by the teacher. One further note which confused me was that Mike's worst subject, and the one in which his teacher was the most dissatisfied with him, was reading.

The next day I called Mike's mother. She was cooperative and offered her assistance in any way that would help Mike. I told her that I was still checking to see what his problems were, and before I set any strategies, I would get back to her. During the conversation, she supplied a singular clue when she said, "He always tells me he doesn't have any homework, but I know it can't be true."

The afternoon of November 18, I saw Mike. In front of me I had jotted a few notes on what I had discovered, and Mike handed me his two-day diary—all eleven pages of it! He had added such details as the times he went to the drinking fountain, and that he had a peanut butter and jelly sandwich before he went to bed. Unfortunately, it took the better part of ten minutes to prune the voluminous report down to specifics. I did this by constantly asking him, "Do you think this helped or hindered your school work?" At the end of the ten minutes I had a skeleton idea of what Mike did with most of his time. Now I was ready to start step one of the five-step program.

The clue provided by his mother plus the fact that nowhere in the diary did he mention taking books home for study showed that the first problem he had was bringing home books and alerting his parents that he had homework. I proposed a program using the PBM Progress Report sheet. (See Chapter 12.) On this sheet each day's classes and assignments were given, initialed by the teacher, by me, and by his mother as he completed each assignment. Even if there was no homework, that had to be indicated too. In the morning, before going to class, he had to bring the sheet to me and receive one for the next day.

This procedure was maintained for the following eight days of the new marking period. Procedures were explained both to Mike and his parents, and within the short span we all began to see results. By the eighth day, he had acquired the habit of automatically taking his books home with all his assignments written down and telling his mother as soon as he arrived. The fact that Mike was turning in homework pleased his teachers, and while his grades were not spectacular, he did manage to pass all required work in these eight days. Mike seemed pleased that he could handle this small task, but before he became complacent it was time to start on the next problem.

This one was a little harder: how not to put off a two-week assignment until the night before. For the first time I asked him if he had any suggestions. He couldn't think of any, but said that he would talk to his mother. The next day he proposed the use of a calendar which his mother would place on his bedroom door. This seemed to solve the second set of problems, but Mike still wasn't internalizing or perpetuating any new study habits of his own. As long as I or his mother directed him, he did what he was told. His class participation was still at a minimum, and he was volunteering no information.

The next problem was to discover why Mike did well in civics but failed the rest of his subjects. We were now three weeks into the new marking period, and while Mike was doing the required work, his classroom attitude showed his lack of interest in everything except civics.

Mike came for a Preventive Conference to discuss the problem. I immediately noted that his attitude was, "What are we going to solve today?" He had come to think that the *PBM* was going to solve his problems. It was time to put the pressure on *him*. With the minimum amount of direction, I asked Mike to analyze what he did in civics class; we got very specific. Making sure that he did not wander from the subject at hand, I called his attention to every statement that he began, "I always do . . ." or "I make sure I . . ." In 15 minutes Mike had a list of the positive things he did in civics class. Just before I dismissed him, I told him to keep the list with him, and we would discuss his other classes next week. At this point I wrote my second observation:

"Mike can be led and acts only upon that which he can use."

The following week I saw Mike and said that we were going to spend the time looking at his other classes. I never mentioned the word comparison, but I asked him to take out the list we had compiled for civics. He had lost the paper, but he remembered what was on it; we quickly wrote it down again. I asked him what he thought his worst subject was, and he said math. I had him describe some of the things he did in math class. Suddenly, about halfway through, he said, "I don't ask enough questions!" Containing myself I said, "What do you mean?" "Well, if I ask questions when I don't know something, then I'll understand it better." Barely breathing I asked, "Are you sure that will work?" "Sure!" he said, "You see, when I ask Mr. Glenn (civics teacher), he tells me where I can look something up, and then I understand it." I wasn't certain that Mike had understood what he had said, but he immediately followed with, "Will Miss James answer me? I don't think she likes me." Knowing that this was a new tool and not wanting him to lose the fervor of his first self-analytic idea, I said, "Why don't you try it out and I'll see you in two days."

I stopped the interview at this high point and alerted Miss James that Mike was going to try out a new tool and waited the two days. The Mike that walked in two days later had found his tool successful and was ready to work out another one. *He* was doing the work now, but he was still looking to me for approval. Eventually, he would be able to stand alone with his new academic success.

If you are the type that is interested in postscripts, Mike never became an A student. He eventually averaged C's with a couple of B's—but that's sure better than D's and F's!

6

How the Referral Factor of
the PBM Plan Works

In Chapter 3 there is an overview given on how to solve
real problems with general categorizing of those real problems.
With this in mind, let's look at the Referral Factor of the PBM
Plan.

WHY STUDENTS ARE REFERRED

The eight types of misconduct which lead to student
referrals answer the question how but not necessarily why a
student misbehaves. Even the five general reasons why most
children misbehave do not answer the specific question of why
Johnny got in trouble. The PBM Plan cannot work in generali-
ties, but only in specifics—hence its name, *Personalized* Behavioral Modification. Now, we must take into account factors that
lead to misconduct but are inherent in only one individual
student.

Missing breakfast may create no problem to four out of
five students but to the fifth, it will change his pattern of
behavior enough to cause him trouble. Confrontations with
parents just prior to the start of the school day can bring
unreleased emotions to the classroom. Being the "new kid on
the block" may make Mary, a normally productive student, an
active classroom disruptor. In other words, for each child the
actions he expresses come from *himself* and *his* surroundings.

In one student, classroom distractions may show a need

for attention from the teacher while in another, the wanted attention may come from peers. Likewise, ripping up a disliked textbook may be an act of rebellion for one student but may have a hidden psychological reason in another. Delving into *why individual* students get into behavioral difficulties is the main task of the PBM Administrator.

HOW TO DEAL WITH THE FIRST REFERRAL

Looking at the behavioral grid (Chapter 4, Figure 4-1), you will note that the three important questions are not loaded; they imply no disapproval or sanction, nor an automatic placing of guilt. For the student who already may feel that he is falsely accused, the manner in which the PBM Administrator begins can set the tone for the entire PBM experience. The first time the PBM Administrator sees a student on a referral, he is a blank slate. He has never been sent before, and anything heard about him previously can only be taken as hearsay. Even if the student has been involved in an Academic Referral, his current behavioral referral must be treated as if he were a stranger. *No* mention of his academic problems can be made. Here again is the definite separation between work and behavioral problems. We cannot stress enough—a student may be succeeding in changing his study habits and still find himself in social behavioral difficulties, but to tie his failure to comply with socially acceptable norms with his previous attempts at educational success can destroy that success. This cannot be permitted.

Let's take two cases, first where the child has been seen before, and then where he has not. The first student we will call Sam. Having worked with him before on an Academic Referral and being human, the PBM Administrator has formed a general analysis of Sam's personality. Remember, however, that he is now in behavioral trouble, a completely different field. Why he is failing math should not and probably does not have any connection with why he slugged Billy. By the same token, the child knows the PBM Administrator and that is a problem. You must always be supportive of *him* but not of his misconduct. If there is a sudden change in attitude toward him because he has a behavioral problem, he will figure that any other showing of concern was a fraud.

Now let's go to Al. Al comes to the PBM Plan because he was fighting on the playground. According to the grid, he accepts his punishment for an authority-oriented reason. The interview proceeds, and the first impression is still mixed. It is not clear if he is stringing you along in order to avoid severe punishment or if he is genuine in his understanding of his responsibilities. As with all conference schedules, check with his teachers before seeing him within a week. But, throughout the interview assume the higher motivation. I usually add a joking comment to let the child know that I am going to look into it. Sometimes stories are changed on the spot! If that is the case, even greater approval is shown that he has told the truth, not a disappointment that at first he lied. *Personal* success for each student comes when he accepts responsibility for *his* own actions (good or bad) and then can *control* his actions.

The problems presented in the first referral should be handled as unique. Each problem must be viewed against the background of that particular incident and the particular student involved. But what happens if the student appears again because of misconduct?

HOW TO IDENTIFY A PATTERN IN REFERRALS

The PBM Administrator does not sprinkle the students in the PBM with any magic powder that instantly ends all their misbehavior after the first time. While it is true that some students only need to be shown how to handle one small incident, most of my students had long histories of behavioral problems. When a child has been referred once, and all pertinent data has been collected (student analysis, teacher's comments, etc.), the material is filed. Should the child appear a second time, start the procedures as if the child is someone you met but cannot quite remember. This is not the time to bring up his past, but merely another chance to help him. Handle the interview exactly the same as it was handled at first, up to the point where student analysis begins. At this point go to the file and say that you want to check your references. The two incidents have not been connected in any other manner except that the same child is involved. Take all pertinent information on the second referral and set up a Preventive Conference within three days. The student is dismissed, and the PBM Administrator's work begins. After checking with his teachers again for this incident, begin to look for similarities between the first and second referral. Do not look for individual why's, but just when's or where's. Even after two referrals, I discovered that I could see such similarities as:

1. Had a substitute.
2. Same teacher involved.
3. Same subject involved.
4. Same time of day.
5. During a test.
6. During group work.
7. Same students involved.
8. Day of the week the same.
9. During assemblies and trips.

These are physical similarities. If the student doesn't conform to these, check the social similarities such as:

1. Group of boys/girls against a girl/boy.
2. Verbalization against authority.
3. Overreaction to the threat of social punishment.
4. To be with the crowd.

Again, there may seem to be no connection. If this is the case, then the conference for the second referral is handled exactly the same way as the first referral; for this too may be a one-time incident.

I would like to add at this point that some of my students were referred more than twice. For these, connecting their behavior in a pattern was made easier by each new incident.

A GUIDE FOR BUILDING AN INDIVIDUALIZED
PROGRAM BASED UPON THE REFERRAL

Before a possible program can be designed for a student, some patterns must be seen. Students do not act in an eclectic manner, even if it appears so.

Suppose you, as a PBM Administrator, are faced with a student who doesn't seem to show any connecting pattern for three referrals. Obviously the child is creating a social problem for himself, but you can't seem to put your finger on why. You have held Preventive Conferences with him after each misconduct, and indeed he has not repeated any of his previous offenses. Do you have to wait until he has tried everything? No. You have been given the clues, but they don't come together. If you are stumped even after talking with his teachers and parents, maybe it is time to see the school psychologist.

Be careful, the rule of confidentiality only allows you to discuss the instances of misconduct and not any of your findings—no specifics like the child's name or any personal facts and statements he might have made. The school psychologist may lead you into avenues that you might not even have considered.

But now, let us assume that a pattern *has* presented itself. You have done your homework; you find the student's problems and most of the reasons. Now is the time to begin to help him change his pattern. The tools given to a student to handle a one-time incident are one thing, but the tools needed to change an outlook are another. In the Academic Achievement Factor, we take the easiest problem first. In the Referral Factor, we take the most *visible* problems first.

For example, if Johnny always fights, changing the aggression to shouting rather than physical force may be the first step. This has not solved his problem of how to cope with a peer, but it is a visible sign both to the student and the teachers/administration that he is trying to change. Indeed, the long-term goal is to have Johnny circumvent the situation entirely, but that takes more self-discipline than he has at this time. If you ask too much, you will get nothing, and you have lost the chance for his success.

Having solved even one glaring problem builds the self-confidence the student needs to exert continuous effort. Again let us compare with the Academic Achievement Factor—an immense amount of self-confidence is built when a student who is failing spelling passes his first spelling test. So, too, confidence is built when a student who is always thrown out by a substitute remains in class for the first time. Keep in mind a few short suggestions:

1. Make the Preventive Conferences close enough together so the student probably will not get into difficulty between them. If you think he can't last three days, hold his conference in two.
2. Remember the age and level of the child with whom you are working. Do not ask an eighth-grader to do something that is too childish for him, or an eight-year-old something that requires great maturity.
3. Be aware of the difficulties the students may have in using the suggestions and tools you give them. It is easy for you to say "Do . . . ," but if it is too difficult for them you have built in failure rather than success.
4. Make all teachers aware that the student is now in the Program. Even though you don't tell them everything, they will be aware and will look for changes in behavior.
5. Use every opportunity to build on past successes. If Georgie gets into difficulty for not raising his hand but he stays in his seat, something he didn't do before, stress the latter and work on the former.
6. Be visibly supportive of all changes toward success. Speaking to a teacher on behalf of a student can show your intent to help in any way you can.
7. Extend the child a little after each success. Do not stretch too far or he might fail, but do not deny his chance for successful social growth by making his tasks too easy. One method for this is the lengthening and shortening of the time span between conferences. For example, if Georgie is learning to stay in his seat, then one conference after two days and another a week after that may be

sufficient. When you start to work on his raising his hand, go back to the two-day schedule.

8. Always inform the student of the strategies and the goals. There will be changes and modifications within the Program as the child gains responsibilities for his own actions, but he should be aware that neither you nor he should lose sight of the goal.

You must get the child actively participating in the changes in patterns. As he succeeds, he begins to internalize. As he internalizes, his need for you and the PBM Plan begins to decrease. Before you release him, however, make certain that his success is permanent. It takes a sense of timing.

"WATCH YOUR TIMING"

Assuming that the steps have been followed and the child seems to be progressing steadily, you do not wish to confine him to the PBM Plan longer than necessary. The goal is self-discipline on the part of the student, and his success leads to his release from the program. "Releasing" means he does not have to report to you on any regular basis. You are not going to check his performance in class. You will no longer be actively involved with his parents, and generally you will act toward him as if he were a member of the general student body. There is a responsibility here: before you release a student you must be as certain as possible that he is ready for all the ramifications of that release.

Why is this so important? The main reason is that once a child is released from the program any misconduct that brings him back to the program can only be construed as a failure. Are there no safeguards? Must it be all or nothing? No. One of the tools instilled in every student is the accessibility of the PBM Administrator. Every student, once he is released from the program, is made aware that he may return for a student-requested conference whenever he feels he needs specific help. There is no failure connected with this action because he is acting on his own; *he* is controlling the situation. How do you know when it is time to release? There are some indications.

A CHECKLIST FOR INDICATiONS OF CHANGE

By making up a list for yourself and the student, you can almost pinpoint the time for release. When I first begin to think about releasing I submit the following form to a student and have him fill it out. (See Figure 6-1.) At the same time, I fill it out using information I have gathered through observation, teacher conferences and student contact. When the child is ready to be released, the two sheets are usually almost identical.

The last step is to pick up all positive indications of change noted in the child's behavior. This information generally comes from the teachers and shows that the student has achieved his goal of continued socially acceptable behavior. The internalization of the new patterns shows that the student is ready to act outside the structure of the PBM. As you can see, there are actually four steps: discovery of the problem; tools for change; reinforcement of change; and self-sufficiency with the solution of the problem. Each one of the cases below indicates a child at various levels. These are not meant to be complete cases, but are illustrative of patterns within the various stages of a conference schedule.

THE CASES OF J., C., R. AND W.

J.–Discovery of the problem.

J. is a seventh-grade boy who was referred to me for "constant and repeated disruption of class by actions and verbalizations. He uses abusive language in class as well as shooting paper clips and rubber bands through the air." Upon asking J. the three questions, I received, "Oh, I was trying to change my seat, and the teacher got all upset." According to the grid this was total nonacceptance and gave definite indications of not being just a one-time difficulty. Since I didn't know J., I had to check with his teachers. All of their comments gave me a picture of a student who was rebellious and openly defiant of authority. He showed no self-discipline and at first indicated no willingness to change. I called his parents and spoke with his

STUDENT'S EVALUATION SHEET

Check the column that most nearly applies. Remember, there are no right or wrong choices, so check what you *really* do.

	Always	Usually	Sometimes	Hardly Ever	Never
1. Raise hand in class					
2. Act up in line					
3. Arrive at class on time					
4. Do what I'm told					
5. Behave when a substitute is in					
6. Talk in class					
7. Write on desks					
8. Lean back in chairs					
9. Chew gum in class					
10. Throw objects in class					
11. Hit other students					
12. Have all materials for class					
13. Help teacher when asked					
14. Act politely					
15. Pay attention in class					
16. Clean up desk area					
17. Accept extra duties in class					
18. Use lavatory time properly					
19. Turn in found objects to teacher or office					
20. Obey safety patrol					
21. Copy work from others					
22. Use abusive language					
23. Destroy property					
24. Take responsibility for my own actions					
25. Seek help if in difficulty					
	Always	Usually	Sometimes	Hardly Ever	Never

FIGURE 6-1

mother. "I just don't understand," she commented. "He has become so uncooperative. Why just yesterday he even swore at his father." There was no need to further classify the type of behavior, only to find out why as quickly as possible.

With the agreement of the administration I lengthened J.'s stay in the PBM Room. During the first two conferences, J. was either vague, noncommittal or openly defiant. However, getting no negative response from me for either action, he finally made a statement: "Why should you care? Nobody else does." That was the key. Going back to the grid, J. now fit in the extreme end of the self-accusatory scale. Before anything else could be accomplished, J. would have to accept himself as a human being of worth.

C.—Tools for change.

C. is a fifth-grade boy whose problem was that he would do almost anything to gain peer acceptance. While not actually a troublemaker he disrupted the class by acting silly. He was aware of his problem but did not know how to solve it. During one of our conferences he stated, "Sometimes it doesn't seem to matter if I act up, but the teacher really gets mad if I do it when the class is working." The tool needed was a way for C. to work quietly when everyone else did. He was told to pick a chair in the back of each one of his classes to which he could move when it was time to work. This action, we both agreed, would show the teacher his intent to try and stay out of trouble, and had the additional benefit of allowing C. to produce greater class work.

This, however, was only part of the solution. Ideally, C. should have been able to work in his own seat. After a few weeks of changing seats, I changed strategy. "C., when do you usually decide to go to your other seat?" He described to me what the teacher said, how the other students acted, and finally how he gathered up his materials and moved to the other chair. We discussed how much time he wasted by having to move. I suggested that he try to work at his desk for a couple of days. Of course, I added, if it didn't work out he should go to the other desk. In two days C. said, "I got my work done!" It was true. He had internalized the suggestion on how to maintain himself in class. The external need for the other desk had disappeared, and C. could work no matter where he sat.

R.—Reinforcement with change.

R. is an eighth-grade girl who is basically peer-oriented. She was prone to disrupting class and getting into difficulties in open-structured situations such as gym, art, assemblies and field trips. While in the program she made considerable effort to use the tools given to her. One of the tools that she had completely internalized was doing things when she was told. She learned to control her actions and ceased her habitual procrastination and back talk. During one conference she told me, "I'm really trying, but one of my teachers won't let up. He is still acting like he did before. You said the teachers would notice the change in my attitude. I'm going to keep it up, but maybe you should talk to him."

Not to accept a direct challenge would have been impossible. R. had complied with everything I asked, and I had to do the same for her. Consequently, I set up an appointment with her teacher.

His comments showed that while he had noticed some changes in R., he still did not feel that she was complying with his standards. I pressed the point that she was trying, and didn't that warrant some tolerance? He did not agree. Finally, I asked him if children needed understanding in order to develop; he said yes. "Well, then," I demanded, "We must give it to R!" Grudgingly he agreed but stipulated that she would have to do much better in his class.

My conference with R. the next day dealt mainly with how she could handle this teacher. I told her of my conference and agreed with her that perhaps he was being a bit unco-operative. I suggested that she work even harder for him, and together we would try to win him over. She was reinforced, but she still had to work.

W.—Self-sufficiency with the solution to the problem.

W. is a sixth-grade boy who first came to me on an Academic Referral but within two days was sent in on a Behavioral Referral. There was a total of four conferences, another referral, three conferences, a parent conference, and three more conferences in the space of 18 weeks. His progress, while rocky in the beginning, had progressively improved. In the past two weeks I had heard nothing but positive statements both by him and about him. I decided to give him the student evaluation sheet to see how he viewed his progress. I had already filled one out on him myself.

He was even harder on himself than he should have been. The growth in his self-control was immense. The next step was to poll his teachers, and I received the following comments:

> "Behavior has been very good. He is attentive and actively participates in class discussion and projects. His marks have also been quite good; his work is satisfactory although he is occasionally talkative; has been very good these past few weeks. I know he's been very concerned about this coming meeting; he is not an outstanding student, but his work has shown a marked improvement in neatness and accuracy; and his behavior is tremendously improved. He listens carefully, follows directions, and obviously tries to maintain his self-control."

Having no fear that he could not sustain his pattern of success. I confidently released W.

J., C., R., and W. are all examples of the various stages in the Referral Factor of the PBM Plan. Although each is shown at only one level, of all the students that I handled within the PBM Plan, all but eleven students reached the point of socially acceptable behavior with its new pattern of success, which W. eventually enjoyed.

The New Option–The In-School Suspension Factor

With the search for new options has come a realization that there are some behavioral problems that still must have a severe punitive consequence. Understanding, patience, consistency of rules and all other positive aids to social growth are still needed, but at some point there must be a punishment for severe noncompliance and misconduct. This may not apply to all students, but there must be something available to deal effectively with the otherwise uncontrollable child.

IN-SCHOOL VS. OUT-OF-SCHOOL SUSPENSION

Having already stated the basic weaknesses in today's use of suspension, let's review the uses for this option. In-school suspension is the next to the last resort, out-of-school being the end of the line. There is nothing more drastic for a school than to admit that it can no longer educate one of its students!

The first step in making this option effective is to make it applicable only to the severest offenses. Time should be spent by administrators, teachers, parents, police and Board of Education members to decide at what point the school is willing to admit defeat. We cannot stress enough that to suspend a student for a minor offense is to remove the very factor in his life that can promote any kind of socially acceptable growth. Once a school has tried all other methods, removal from the general student body is the *final* option.

Let's look at some offenses which administrators agree are suspendible:

1. Smoking.
2. Using excessive force on another student.
3. Striking a teacher or an administrator or using uncontrolled, abusive language.
4. Wanton cutting of classes, truancy, or tardiness.
5. Releasing fire crackers, turning in fire alarms, vandalism.
6. Community offenses requiring court appearance.

As far as the PBM Plan is concerned, all of the above offenses are *In-School Suspension* offenses. Naturally, something must be done with these students, but they should not be denied the possibility of a controlled, structured and supportive instructional base. Imagine the harm that can be done to an incorrigible runaway whose only connection to a structured environment is the school, if the school puts him on the street. We have no intention of turning our schools into child correctional centers, but a little common sense must be exercised before we throw away the school as a viable force in a child's life. At the present time, the schools have no way of handling these students; the PBM Plan is an answer.

Should out-of-school suspension ever be used? Yes, perhaps. In the ten years I have been in the classroom, I found three or four students who presented such a threat to themselves and the school as to warrant their removal. Extortion at the point of a weapon, rape, overt sociopathic displays, pushing drugs–these are the types of offenses which call for the school to remand the student to other resources in our society. In an elementary school particularly, to suspend a child from school for disrupting the nurse's office can place a stigma on his educational growth which may never be erased. Our schools are learning centers at all levels; we must use them.

When the school has decided on what are suspendible offenses, the list may be nothing like the one cited. Yours must reflect your community and your school. In the hierarchy of misbehavior, a Preventive Conference should be used when a rule is broken that states, "You *should* not"; a Referral for the breaking of a rule stated as, "You *may* not"; In-School Suspension for a rule that states, "You *will* not"; and out-of-school suspension for rules that are stated, *"You must never—ever!"*

WHEN TO USE IN-SCHOOL SUSPENSION

Once it has been decided *precisely* what are suspendible offenses for your school, there must be consistency. There are times when a teacher or an administrator can lessen a referable offense and merely call for a Requested Conference. This can *never* be the case when faced with the decision to place the child on In-School Suspension. He either has committed one of the named offenses or he has not. No other type of offense can be elevated to the level of an In-School Suspension, nor any of your stated offenses lessened by mitigating circumstances. It must never be used as a threat. Prospective law officers presumably are told never to draw their guns unless they expect to use them. The same is true for this punitive weapon: using it as a threat diminishes its effectiveness. Students respect boundaries if they are well defined, and In-School Suspension should stand like a brick wall. One essential benefit to teachers and administration in maintaining this posture is that no emotion need sway their decisions. If a child has committed a suspendible infraction he is suspended.

One caution: do not make the mistake of adding cumulative behavior to the list of suspendible offenses. X number of referrals does not equal an In-School Suspension; X number of in-school suspensions does not equal an out-of-school suspension.

As stated earlier the PBM Plan is practical. These theories of In-School Suspension are the results of extended involvement with severe behavioral problems. The only things added to the common practice of suspension are common sense, consistency, a clear definition of offenses and a firm footing for all those who wish to use this option. No parents can now rush into the office irate over their child's suspension. With this plan, the answer is clear: your child did X, X is a suspendible offense, and therefore he is suspended.

There is no reason why types of misconduct cannot be added or subtracted from the list. If this is done, however, be sure that the student body, parents, and teachers have been well informed.

Penalties are mutually agreed upon at all educational levels. Smoking may be determined to be a two-day offense while wanton destruction of property may incur a five-day penalty. Periodic review of these offenses and penalties will add relevance to the new option.

Now, given the In-School Suspension factor is clearly defined, how does the Plan deal with the suspended student?

HOW TO DEAL WITH THE SUSPENDED STUDENT

At this point in the In-School Suspension factor of the PBM Plan, the PBM Administrator does not seek rehabilitation, but containment. Let us assume that the child has been removed for a major act of vandalism: he jumped up and down on a sink in the boy's room until it collapsed, and he's caught in the act. He is brought to the main office where he is read the rule, informed that his parents will be notified and (depending on the school) may have to pay for the damage, and that he is now suspended. He is then brought, preferably in silence, to the PBM Room where a copy of the offense and the length of the In-School Suspension are given to the PBM Administrator.

The PBM Administrator places the student in a seat in the In-School Suspension Area, reads him the rules of the room, and has the student fill out a Schedule Form. (See Figure 7-1.) When this has been completed the student may be asked to perform some time-consuming task until the PBM Administrator has notified all teachers involved and received books and classroom assignments for the rest of the day. The student remains in the PBM Room at all times.

Date: _____

This is to inform you that _____ will not be present in

following classes. Please initial and return to me.

1. _____

2. _____

3. _____

4. _____

5. _____

6. _____

7. _____

Please supply all work to be done by the student today. If there are any questions, please state them on the back of this sheet. Thank you.

FIGURE 7-1

94

Date: _Oct 2_

This is to inform you that _Don Mannix_ will not be present in the

following classes. Please initial and return to me.

1. Music – Griffins – Copy all songs + signatures in Chapter 2 – Study for Test 10/3 _LG_

2. English – Adams – pp. 38-42. Do Ex. A - Ex. B+C for homework. _G.A._

3. Geography – Davis – Unit 5 - Indonesia ques 1-20 Pg 57 _FD_

4. Math – Magalisco – ex. 4-7 pp. 84-86 Show all work . no homework _CM_

5. Science – Blake – Do worksheets 6+7, if not finished do for homework _DB_

6. Gym – Soleman – Read Chapter 2 in Health Book _(BS)_

7. History – Lang – Outline Chapter 3 in paragraph form _RL_.

Please supply all work to be done by the student today. If there are any questions, please
state them on the back of this sheet. Thank you.

FIGURE 7-2

As class work is completed (Figure 7-2), it is given to the teachers at the time the student would actually be in class. It must be stressed that while the student does not participate in any of the social aspects of school (going to class, assemblies, activities, etc.), he is responsible for all the academic aspects (assignments, homework, tests, etc.). The student has committed an anti-social act; consequently he is removed from the *social,* but *not* the *academic,* aspects of school.

Certain privileges must be maintained, but they too lose their social aspect. A student is permitted to go to the lavatory or the nurse's office if he requests it, but must be accompanied. If it is to the lavatory, he is given the shortest reasonable amount of time to be gone; if to the nurse, he must get a note from the nurse describing the nature of his complaint. If his illness is such that he must be sent home for any remaining part of the day, the time must be made up at the end of the In-School Suspension.

One further note on making up days: if a child goes home for lunch and decides not to come back for the afternoon or if he does not come to school for any of the days of the suspension, the time is added. If the length of an In-School Suspension is five days, then five days are served.

Dismissal from school at the end of the school day is done from the PBM Room, and the child is escorted to the nearest exit. The next morning he reports to the PBM Room again. All gathering of homework assignments, attendance, forms, etc., is handled by the PBM Administrator, not by the student. The cutoff from the school's social environment must be complete.

Once the suspended student has served the time of an In-School Suspension, the PBM Administrator can switch to a different posture. Now she can begin to analyze the student's problems and begin to support him constructively.

HOW TO ANALYZE THE STUDENT'S BEHAVIOR

Generally, the PBM Administrator has plenty of time to

gather data concerning the suspended student. Daily contact with his teachers, feedback on whether he is complying with classroom assignments while on suspension, and previous files on the student are all sources from which the PBM Administrator can draw. Given that there are some isolated instances where a suspendible offense is not the student's general behavior but a one-time occurrence, usually there are other examples of nonacceptable behavior. Let's take both cases.

Mary, a fifth-grade girl, had no prior connection with the PBM Plan before she became involved in a brawl on the playground. She struck another student repeatedly while sitting on top of him; even when a teacher tried to intervene, Mary remained uncontrolled. Mary's teachers, however, characterized her as a rather good student, a bit spirited, but causing no real difficulty. What had caused the emotional display on the playground was a rather obscene observation on the sexual proclivities of her mother. Her fit of temper, while inexcusable since it represented a threat to another student, was understandable: she thought she was protecting the honor of her mother. The PBM Administrator's task would be to agree with the motive, but to suggest another method of acting upon it in the future.

But what of Michael, an eighth-grade boy? He was told to leave the gym, for disrupting a class. Screaming at the teacher that he wasn't going to the office and there wasn't a thing the teacher could do about it, Michael picked up a baseball and threw it at the teacher. Michael was known to the PBM and, indeed, had caused several other disruptions in classes. His progress in the PBM was not sustained, and a great deal of work still had to be done. Here, the suspendible offense was an extension of a noted pattern of behavior. During the suspension, Michael found it difficult to comply with the requirements; his teachers were not satisfied either with his work or his behavior. The files on Michael showed that his misconduct was motivated in the same manner as his previous offenses.

Here then are two types of students. How they are handled after the suspension is as important, if not more so, than the suspension itself.

HOW TO TRANSFER THE SUSPENDED STUDENT
TO A PREVENTIVE CONFERENCE SCHEDULE

The key to this step is timing. For the duration of the suspension the PBM Administrator is the container, or as one of my students put it, "The Warden." Shortly (perhaps 20 minutes) before the suspension is over, however, the PBM Administrator begins to change the atmosphere. Statements about how difficult it is to sit in an In-School Suspension and how much better it is to be in class cause the student to begin thinking about adjusting his behavior. Calling the student from the In-School Suspension Area to the Preventive Conference desk, the PBM Administrator and the student begin to use the Preventive Conference Factor of the PBM Plan.

There are some modifications: first, no excuses, rationalizations, or explanations are acceptable. As it was in the principal's office, the suspendible act was either committed or it wasn't. What the PBM Administrator is interested in is whether or not the student knows *why* the incident took place. Second, while usually there is a reinforcement of the teacher's classroom management, in this case the PBM Administrator reinforces the administration's role and the school rules. Third, incidents in Preventive Conferences are usually taken separately with different conferences for academic and behavioral problems; but after an In-School Suspension, the student is dealt with in his entirety: his work process is analyzed as well as his behavior. This does not violate PBM's separation of work and punishment, for the student must now be made to view *all* aspects of his role as a student. Fourth and finally, if the student is uncooperative or displays any unacceptable behavior during this first conference, the PBM Administrator might decide not to return the student to class, not as a punishment but as a prevention of further possible difficulties for the student. The suspended student is very susceptible to teasing from his peers and is usually defensive toward his teachers. If he is not prepared to return to class, he is only heading for more difficulty. If the PBM Administrator senses this, a further conference the following day might aid the student's transition back to class.

The intent of an In-School Suspension is to punish severe misbehavior; the primary goal of the PBM Plan, however, is the prevention of future misconduct and the strengthening of self-discipline. The suspended student needs a great deal of support. Once having decided that the student may return to class, the Administrator should hold a conference with him at the end of his first full day. In this way, the PBM Plan begins immediately to aid the student and to reinforce whatever success he may have found in the transition. Seeing the suspended student on a Preventive Conference Schedule frequently during the first two weeks after a suspension not only prevents any future misconduct but also prevents his feeling that he was "bad." Help given precisely when needed is remembered and acted upon later.

GUIDELINES FOR EVALUATION

Evaluating the effectiveness of the In-School Suspension factor must occur on two levels, first in terms of the program itself, and second in terms of the students involved. Let's look at the steps for each evaluation.

In terms of the Program, the In-School Suspension factor of the PBM Plan is effective if:

1. The number of suspended students goes down.
2. The repetition of suspendible offenses goes down.
3. The seriousness of the suspendible offenses goes down.
4. Disassociation of chronic student behavioral problems goes down.
5. The productivity of the suspended students goes up.
6. Faculty support and confidence go up.
7. Parental understanding and support go up.
8. The Administrator's role is strengthened.

The benefits the administration gains through the use of the In-School Suspension factor can be readily measured by these eight criteria. More intangible but just as important are the benefits of more consistent punitive options, more control over student misconduct, and more cohesive understanding between students, teachers, and administrators with no appreciable increase in any of their work loads. The administrator and the teacher are not "punished" by having the suspended student remain in school, and the student does not receive the "reward" of a vacation after a severe misconduct.

In terms of the student, the In-School Suspension factor of the PBM Plan is effective if:

1. The repetition of suspendible offenses goes down.
2. The connection between action and consequence is strengthened.
3. Student re-entry into classes is made easier and more successful.
4. The loss of educational time is substantially decreased.
5. Student appreciation and understanding of the boundaries of proper conduct is strengthened.
6. Student willingness to comply with school rules is increased.
7. The hero mystique of the suspended student is eliminated.

Here again, there are some intangible benefits for the students. Emphasis is placed on the fact that while his misbehavior will not be tolerated, *he has worth*. The support he receives from the PBM Plan causes him to feel that he is still a part of the school. Finally, he gains a greater respect for the system because it reacts fairly and consistently.

A CASE OF "SMOKING IN THE BOY'S ROOM"

Let's say that on the list of suspendible offenses is smoking in or around the school building. At 9:14 a.m. Mr. Davies, a math teacher, walks into the boy's bathroom to discover an eighth-grade student, Don Mannix, leaning against a sink and smoking a cigarette. Quickly, Don tries to drop the cigarette, realizes that he is caught and begins trying to convince Mr. Davies not to turn him in. Mr. Davies refuses and takes Don to the office. The trip down the hallway becomes noisy as Don begins ranting abusively to the teacher.

After they arrive at the office and Mr. Davies tells his story, the principal turns to Don and asks, "Were you smoking in the boy's room?"

"I don't see what the big deal is! One lousy cig . . ."

"Were you smoking in the boy's room?"

"Yeah," Don finally admits.

"Smoking in or around the school building," the principal continues without raising his voice, "is punishable by an in-school suspension lasting three days. As of this moment you are on In-School Suspension. Mr. Davies, will you please fill out this form and escort Don to the PBM Room?" At 9:31 a.m. Don enters the PBM Room.

"So what happens now?" Don shrugs as he enters the room.

"The first thing that happens, Mr. Mannix," says Mrs. Greene, the PBM Administrator, "is that you sit in that chair and listen—listen very closely while I read you the rules of the room." When she has finished, she asks Don if he understands.

"Yeah."

"I beg your pardon, Mr. Mannix, what did you say?"

"I said yeah!"

"I beg your pardon, Mr. Mannix, what did you say?"

"Yes, Mrs. Greene."

"Thank you, Mr. Mannix. Please remember to address me properly whenever you speak to me."

Mrs. Greene now hands Don the Schedule Form and tells him to fill it out, listing all the classes he has that day. (See Figure 7-2.) Don complies and returns the form to Mrs. Greene, who asks a student runner to deliver Don's schedule to the teachers involved. While waiting for the assignments to arrive, Don is given the task of copying an assignment for another student. At 9:46 Don's first assignment arrives. By 10:09 all of his assignments for the day and his homework for that night have arrived, and Don begins working.

At 11:17 Don stands and, having been given permission, asks to go to the lavatory. Mrs. Greene obtains a free male teacher and Don is escorted there, being told that he must return in five minutes. Don returns and the morning progresses until it is time to leave for lunch. There are two other students in the PBM Room, and they are told to report to their homerooms to be dismissed. Don remains in the room; he is dismissed by Mrs. Greene and told to report directly to her that afternoon. The afternoon progresses until ten minutes before the end of school. Don is told to list his homework assignments, gather the necessary books, straighten his desk area and fill out tomorrow's schedule. At the end of school he is dismissed by Mrs. Greene, who escorts him to the door of the school.

The remaining two days progress in much the same manner. Don's homework is sent to his teachers who return Don's assignments for that day.

About 20 minutes before the end of school on the final day of Don's suspension, Mrs. Greene calls Don to her desk.

"Boring, wasn't it?" she remarks. "You know, Don, there's got to be a better way to get an education."

"There sure does! This is the dumbest three days I've ever spent. All you do in here is work!"

"How do you feel about smoking in school?"

"Well, Mrs. Greene, I still like to smoke, but I'm not so sure it's worth all this."

"What do you think about going back to class?"

"It shouldn't be too bad. I got my work done, and I did all my homework. It shouldn't be too tough."

"Don't take it too lightly, Don," continues Mrs. Greene. "You have been out of class for three days. You don't want to get in trouble again, so just take it slowly for the first day. I'm giving you an appointment for tomorrow afternoon so we can check how everything goes. All you have to do is stay in class and do your work, and we'll work the rest out later."

In the three days that Don has been suspended, he has continued his education, has begun to accept responsibility for his actions, and has been started on the path to any help he may need in the future. He has begun to learn.

8

Selecting the PBM
Administrator

Having decided to implement the PBM Plan in your school,
you must now select a PBM Administrator. This chapter
explains and examines the nuances that can spell success or
failure for the Administrator chosen.

WHY THE "RIGHT" ONE IS IMPORTANT

In a real sense, the PBM Administrator *is* the PBM program
in your school. Its success or failure depends upon the interac-
tion of its administrator and the students, faculty and building
administrators. If the PBM Administrator has a personal axe to
grind, the students will quickly discover it and ignore anything
he or she says. If the faculty and building administrator cannot
get along with the PBM Administrator, it is unlikely they will
accept any suggestions that might be made. There is a tightrope
between these three levels of the educational structure that
experienced educators realize is very difficult to walk. This will
be easier, certainly, with the "right" PBM Administrator.

The PBM Administrator has only one goal and purpose—
the reduction of student behavioral problems. Problems must be
dealt with wherever and whenever they are found, and handling
them effectively within the PBM Plan demands consistency.
Sometimes this demand must come directly from the PBM
Administrator; for example, one of my students in the program
got into difficulty and totally lost control in front of the

103

vice-principal who, in turn, became angry and began procedures for out-of-school suspension. When the student came to the PBM Room to wait for his parents to take him home, I questioned him about his misconduct. The offense was not one of the accepted reasons for out-of-school suspension, but one which called for In-School Suspension. I went to the vice-principal's office, and we worked out a satisfactory ending to the incident. This could not have been possible, however, if a strong rapport had not existed between the building and PBM Administrators.

We have seen how each step of the program works and how important the first meeting between the PBM Administrator and the student is toward the successful change in the student's behavior. So much depends upon this first approach that the first PBM Administrator will set the tenor for the entire program for as long as it exists in the school. It is possible to change administrators only if you start out with a good first choice. One can go from good to better but it is impossible, considering the need for trust and harmony, to make the program successful if the first administrator is a poor one. The students never trust the Program again, the faculty either pounces on its weaknesses or ignores it entirely, and the building administrator might attempt to dominate it.

Without the balance maintained by the PBM Administrator, the PBM program will not be effective. Choose carefully, however, and you are on the way to success.

HOW TO PICK A WINNER

Selecting the "right" PBM Administrator may take some time, but the benefits are well worth the effort. When looking, pick a winner. He or she should be dynamic, resourceful and must have "something extra." There's no way to describe this, but if you mentally look over your faculty, aren't there some people to whom both students and other teachers gravitate? It doesn't matter what age or sex they are or if it is their second or forty-second year in teaching—they're special!

There are certain things to look for in a PBM Administrator. The most important quality is a genuine liking for children any age, size or color, just so long as they are children. A second quality is the desire for reform; the Administrator must not be a chronic complainer with no solutions but a searcher for a better way. "It's always been done this way" means nothing to him. Strong principles, a sense of purpose, and a driving desire for excellence make him rail against injustice, prejudice, and mediocrity; he is not complacent, nor does he want things handed to him. The PBM Administrator is not a talker but a doer. A third quality is that he or she must be a "plainclothes teacher"; the term, taken from police terminology, means "not in uniform." The "plainclothes teacher" needs no room or special subject matter: teaching isn't only a profession; it's a way of life. He or she teaches instinctively, whether it be the English Kings, fairness on the playground or the joy of living.

Some other qualities like patience, understanding, a sense of humor, loyalty and self-discipline will stand the PBM Administrator in good stead. This then, is a "winner!" Of course, a possible reaction might be: "Good grief! She's looking for a combined reincarnation of Joan of Arc, Socrates and the Flying Nun!" Not at all! Each of us has these qualities to some extent. Drawing upon them to their fullest is what makes the PBM Administrator unique.

In choosing the first PBM Administrator, seek the one with that "something extra"; that's the winner. The PBM Plan will change your school and you will see its qualities reflected throughout the building. Pick a winner and you are securely on the path to successful educational growth.

HOW TO DETERMINE IF YOU CAN DO IT

Running the PBM Plan, however, is not just a popularity contest; there are certain skills needed. These skills can be developed, but you must have some ability in them to run the

PBM Plan effectively. To determine your ability, check your aptitude in the following skills:

1. Keeping anecdotal records.

Without this ability, watching patterns develop and change is impossible. An anecdotal study is a test of *objective* observation. The key word is "objective": you cannot include in this recording process your feelings toward a student or a behavior. Once you have trained yourself, you should be able to write: "Yesterday, I saw M_____. He smiled, chatted and answered my questions directly. Today, his clothes were disheveled, he did not look directly at me, and he mumbled when answering questions." Obviously, something has changed, but any interjection of your own only clouds the issue. Can you keep your objectivity and write complete and accurate anecdotal records?

2. Teaching multiple subjects on multiple levels.

There may be times in the PBM Room when you are faced with three or more students. Each of these students may be there either for work or behavioral difficulties, and their ages may range from six to fifteen in a K-8 school. The ability to handle each child on his level of understanding and ability is not easy to develop. I found it very difficult: I was used to working with one particular age group and was then faced with "little ones!" My *Human Growth and Development* textbook became dog-eared! Can you picture yourself helping a first-grader with spelling, a fourth-grader with a behavioral problem and a seventh-grader with science?

3. Communicating ideas precisely.

Few of us always say precisely what we mean. The clear communication of thoughts is both a skill and an art; communication of the spoken and written word, however, is vital to the

PBM Plan. There will be situations that call for careful choosing of words in the composition of letters and reports. When composing a letter to a parent, can you write a warning about impending disastrous behavior as if it were a plea for help and not a condemnation? Can you compose a letter of praise for the social or educational growth of a child in such a way that the parents and child keep trying instead of relaxing? Can you write a clear report either to the building administrator or to one of the specialists which explains your findings without breaking the PBM Plan rule of confidentiality?

The spoken word is even more difficult to master. We may say the right thing to someone, but may be misunderstood from poor inflection. If the PBM Administrator is to be effective, he must be a master of the spoken word. There is a modern term in our language called "rapping": to "rap" with someone is to establish complete rapport and communication. This ability to speak to children or adults, to make yourself understood and perhaps even more importantly, to be believed, is your greatest asset. Can you reprimand a second-grader who's been removed from an assembly and comes to you in tears? Can you calm an irate teacher and solicit help with a difficult student? Can you "psyche up" a student who feels he can't succeed to the point where he is ready to return to class and try again?

If you have answered these questions "yes" or even "I think I can," then you indeed may be able to run the PBM Plan in your school.

WORKING ON THE SIDELINES

Having talked about character traits and skills, let's examine the day-to-day work of the PBM Administrator in the school situation. The PBM Administrator must be omnipresent yet invisible: on the one hand, he or she must have style, flair, affability and an active interest in the school; on the other hand, the work of the PBM Administrator must be as a quiet breeze, barely felt and unobtrusive. When dealing with the

program, the Administrator is constantly working on the side-
lines and behind the scenes.

Let's take a couple of examples and explain. Take the
faculty: you must work with them, your personality must be
cheerful and friendly, and you must appear as if you haven't a
care in the world. By the same token, you must involve the
faculty in the PBM Plan. At this point you are serious,
dedicated, professional—and a loner. For the students you must
have the ability to come and go in any part of the school and be
welcome; there should be no dread connected with seeing you.
On the other hand, you must be able to control the students
within the framework of the Program. These balances, while
difficult, are not impossible if you keep some things in mind.

First, who is running the Program, and what is your goal?
For the smooth running of the PBM Plan there can be no
"boss" in the strict sense of the word. Before the Program is
implemented, the PBM and building administrators work out
guidelines and expectations, but each works independently
from the other. The building administrator makes suggestions; it
is, of course, his right to do so. But these suggestions cannot be
so demanding as to rule out compromise. The PBM Administrator also makes suggestions, and the building administrator
must also be willing to compromise. The goal of the Program is
the measurable reduction of student behavioral problems. Working together, the administrators are a team with one common
goal. Strength of purpose makes this a working coalition and
not a struggle for power.

Second, are you a member of the faculty or administration? Actually, the PBM Administrator is neither and both. He
has no duties of teachers or any responsibilities of an administrator. Still, he is somewhere between, with one foot planted
firmly in the classroom and its problems and the other resting
with the administration and its difficulties. The PBM Administrator cannot be such an outsider to the faculty that he is
ignored, but not such an equal that they will not be open to
suggestion. The PBM Plan is in your school to help not just one

group or another, but the whole school. Consequently, there can be no singular allegiance.

Third, what is your role with the students? One of my children once asked me if I was a spy for the teachers. Indeed, the PBM Administrator is not a spy for anyone; the PBM Plan does not pit students against teachers, administrators against students or parents against them all. You are not such a friend that the students always appear in the right, nor are they always wrong. The student's view of the PBM Room should not be a courtroom, but rather a library. Information, help, support and structure are your reasons for being there; step beyond those bounds and you will lose your equilibrium. You cannot fight their battles, but merely point out to them their weaknesses and strengths. You are not their buddy, mother or father, brother or sister, but an adult who wants to assist in their growth.

TWO EXAMPLES: POSITIVE AND NEGATIVE

We cannot stress enough the importance of the PBM Administrator. You have seen the qualifications necessary; now let's look at two interviews, hirings and the subsequent results.

Ms. I.M. Goode

As she enters the school for her interview, Ms. Goode asks a child where the office is located. She is smiling, and as she walks away the child smiles after her. Showing almost no nervousness, she seats herself comfortably as the interview begins. She answers all questions directly and without quibbling. Her credentials are in order and the interview moves along on the format of "What would you do if . . ." questions. Most answers conform to what you think she should do, but one is not even close: you challenge her, and instead of backing down, you find yourself discussing the possibility of doing it her way. As the conversation progresses, she agrees with some of your points and shows no sense of triumph when she has persuaded you to her point of view.

As the interview continues, a teacher interrupts. You introduce Ms. Goode and find her courteous and friendly. There is something else though; it is a meeting of equals.

In a short time the interview is completed and you decide to hire Ms. Goode. During the acclimation period Ms. Goode blends smoothly into the school; she is direct and open and has become acquainted with several members of the faculty. The procedures for the PBM Plan are worked out smoothly, and soon she receives her first candidate. The incident is handled quickly and efficiently. When you see her in the hall to question her as to how it went, you are met with a noncommittal, "Fine"—no explanation, no discussion. She offers, however, to give you a written report if you want one. Just as a check, you go to the teacher who referred the candidate to see how the initiation of the PBM Plan has worked. The teacher shows you the class forms sent from the PBM Room and informs you that the student already has his work. It has run well.

Skipping several months, let's see how Ms. Goode is progressing. Using her talents in art, she has become involved with the art teacher in a poster campaign against drugs; she has helped several teachers design sets for class plays and is working on art designs for the PTA yearbook. Her reports are coming in regularly, the students are showing definite signs of progress, and the faculty seems pleased with the new program. Parent conferences run smoothly, and you are beginning to forget what it was like before the PBM Plan. One thing does strike you funny: the custodian asks you what he is supposed to do with the two sinks he ordered. Every year by this time he would have had to replace the ones that the students ripped off the walls; this year they are still intact. What does he do with the extras? Your PBM Plan is a success, and you have picked a "winner!"

Ms. U.R. Wronge

On the day of the interview, Ms. Wronge arrives precisely on time. She is well dressed, and her credentials are in order. The interview proceeds smoothly until you begin to mention real-life situations. Your opinions coincide so closely that there is no discussion. Only when you play devil's advocate to the extreme does she voice an opinion of her own. You attribute this acquiescence to her desire to please you and not to a weakness. The interview concludes shortly, and you decide to hire her. During the acclimation period you find her willing to do your bidding. She has made several friends on the faculty and seems to be getting along well. Soon an incident arises and she receives her first candidate. When you look into the PBM Room you find the child quietly working. Upon seeing you, Ms. Wronge tells you exactly what has transpired between her and the child. You ask if she has notified the teacher, and she replies "No, not yet."

Again, let's skip several months and see how Ms. Wronge and the PBM are doing. You are still handling most of the behavioral problems through your office. The PBM Room is being used merely for containment. Ms. Wronge and the PBM Plan have not made any measurable differences in your school and there seems very little chance for change. The dynamic, new practical solution has turned out to be a stagnant addition instead.

The major difference in these two examples is that "something extra"—call it confidence, resourcefulness, creativity, or even as the commercials say, "pizazz"—it will make all the difference in the world to PBM. Hire carefully, and success is insured.

"REMEMBER WHEN"—A CHECKLIST FOR SELECTION

When we discussed the qualifications and "extras" of the PBM Administrator, we purposely left out this section. As I speak to groups about the PBM, I am forever captivated by the extra which I call the "Peter Pan Principle." If you remember the musical, you will recall a song entitled "I Won't Grow Up!" It is a declaration never to forget what it means to be a child. This doesn't mean acting like a child, but rather being in the state of perpetual wonder found in childhood.

You must remember when you were a child—not as a

careless observer from the distance of time, but as an active participant in events that just happened. Do this and empathy will color your relationships with the children with whom you will deal. I personally have no trouble empathizing with a misbehaving student. As a youngster, I was in the principal's office so often they used to call it "Sue's Room." Seriously, I remember being thrown out of classrooms, being lectured by teachers and threatened by administrators. I remember the noisy encounters with my parents after each misconduct and how difficult it was to let a fellow student get away with something just for the sake of avoiding some punishment.

This is not to say that a person must have been a terror in his or her youth to be an effective PBM Aministrator, but the angelic honor student whose entire experience with misconduct was not saying "please" and "thank you" may have a hard time relating to some of the students in the PBM Plan.

To see if you have this ineffable extra, let us give you some situations to test your memory. Take some time and really try to remember when . . .

1. You were rebuked by a teacher in front of the whole class.
2. Somebody you really liked said, "I dare you."
3. You walked into class and didn't have your homework.
4. You told the truth and no one believed you.
5. You got blamed for something someone else did.

If you can remember some or all of these, then right now, right this minute, your empathy is working at the level you must maintain when you are talking to the students in the PBM Plan. That feeling you have will carry over and make your suggestions carry the full weight of reality and understanding.

THE FOUR E'S—YOUR BLUEPRINT FOR SUCCESS

The Four E's—Empathy, Enthusiasm, Energy, and Efficiency—are the cornerstones of your success as a PBM Administrator. Without each of these, the PBM Plan might fail.

In the last section we dealt with empathy. The reason for empathy is obvious: if you cannot relate to the students, you will never be able to reach or help them. But, what of the other qualities? Enthusiasm is the faith and belief of a zealot; you must believe that PBM will change your school for the better. Your enthusiasm builds confidence in the students with whom you come in contact, but more importantly, it adds to your dealings with the administration and faculty. You're selling a product—success. Consequently, you must project the feeling of success whenever you speak or act in the PBM Plan. As an example, imagine a Preventive Conference in which you are trying to bolster a young boy's confidence in his teacher's ability to handle a bully. You, personally, must believe that the teacher can do this and must also convince the student. Enthusiasm is your tool. If you are trying to persuade a potential dropout to stay in school, you must be enthusiastic toward school yourself, not with platitudes about getting better jobs or making more money but with a belief that formal education *can* do something for the student; you believe he *will* be better if he stays. The coupling of empathy and enthusiasm in relating to those around you is an unbeatable combination. Even when dealing with faculty members your confidence in the program, your understanding of their problems and your enthusiasm at the prospect of change make the PBM Plan capable of realizing that change. This all requires another E—Energy!

Energy in the PBM Plan is a quality of tirelessness; you are never too busy to take on one more thing. Regardless of how you feel personally, the work of the PBM Plan goes on. You must give the impression that any problem will be given your attention immediately. The only situations you are going to meet are difficulties that have been turned over to you. Therefore, you must be physically and mentally prepared to handle them. This energy, while not as difficult as it sounds, must be present in the personality makeup of the PBM Administrator or the vitality of the Program itself could be lost. "But," you say, "how can a person do five things at once, be resourceful, be ever available to problems?" The answer is the fourth E—Efficiency.

There is a saying that "the journey to Mecca begins with the first step." The moment you begin, you institute procedures for handling the Program. These procedures, carefully planned, will carry you from one situation to another. At one point in the program I was handling 87 students; that is not impossible, but it would have been if it were not done efficiently. You must learn to schedule the necessary facets of the PBM Plan—Preventive Conference, Building Administrative Meetings, interviews with school specialists—in such a way that they can be handled within the framework of those things you can't plan—Teacher-Requested Conferences, In-School-Suspension, Referrals. The ways in which you do this are outlined under each section. This scheduling, along with accurate record keeping and proper management of the PBM Room, spells efficiency and self-discipline. If you keep this last E working for you, the load of the PBM Plan will not be such a burden.

Remember what it is like to be in the student's situation, show them that you believe in them and yourself, understand what is difficult for them to do, have a command over facts and data, and you have guaranteed the successful operation of the PBM Plan.

9

How to Individualize the PBM Plan

Throughout the PBM Plan, the primary concern is the student and the relationship he has with his social and educational environment. It is a concept which the PBM Administrator reinforces toward successful understanding. Each student is made to feel that the Program is working just for him. This feeling of one-to-one is a strong point in the PBM Plan. Even in a group situation, as you will see in this chapter, the PBM Administrator's concern must be for the individual.

INITIAL CONTACT—THE FIRST INTERVIEW

Whenever we meet someone for the first time, be it child or adult, we try to make a good impression. We make our manner pleasant and our voice positive; we assume that we are going to like the stranger, and that the stranger will like us. Unless it is obvious, such as a new teacher being introduced to the principal or a new student being introduced to the teacher, a disparity in position does not matter at the time of the first introduction.

Sometimes adults forget this when dealing with children. A neighbor's daughter once asked if I knew how hard it was to be a child. Her complaint wasn't social—it was physical! Things in easy reach of an adult, for example, were too high for her. Her remark led me to an interesting observation.

The next time you see your principal or a fellow teacher, squat down and sit on your heels. Now listen as the person speaks to you. He sounds ominous, doesn't he? Yet this is the level from which children hear everything you say. Everyone is bigger than they are, can do more things than they can, and knows more than they do—or so it seems.

The PBM Administrator strives for equality and empathy with the children in the Program; this must be established in the first interview. Yes, the PBM Administrator is an adult, but also the PBM Administrator knows what it is like to be a child. The first inkling a child has of this is by the way you say "hello." If you sense that the child is frightened, calm his fear; if he is angry, mollify him until he's rational; if he is crying, give him a Kleenex and a little time to control himself.

The teacher or whoever has sent him has given you a reason why he was sent, but before you can handle the situation, the child before you must become a real person, someone tangible. You must become real to the student as well; he *must* believe that you know *him,* and that you are going to help *him.*

CHECKLIST FOR IDENTIFYING THE PROBLEM

There are obstacles which may hamper building the necessary rapport. If you are aware of them, however, they need not be insurmountable. When a child comes to the PBM Room for the first time, certain of his preconceived notions must be considered: if he is sent for a Preventive Conference or Academic Referral, he may be confused; he may feel he is being punished, but can't pinpoint why. One boy came to me for a Preventive Conference because he was not doing his homework. He was a perfectly good student in no behavioral difficulty, but the teacher felt that I perhaps could increase his productivity in homework. The boy was convinced that he was going to be punished, but the only thing that he could think he had done wrong that day was that he didn't wash his hands when he went to the lavatory!

This first-grader illustrates a real problem in misunderstanding the PBM Administrator's role; another student might come to the PBM Room filled with anxiety or anger over impending punishment. One such student came to me after being removed from an assembly. He had become fidgety and the teacher, realizing that his boredom might eventually lead to trouble, sent him to the PBM Room. Rightfully feeling that he had done nothing wrong, the boy could not understand why he had to stay in the room for three days and why his parents had to be called. Where did he get such an idea? That's what happened to one of his classmates. His preconceived idea was not only erroneous, but if he had verbalized this anger to his teacher, he could have been in more trouble.

One last problem—sometimes teachers, in a genuine effort to show the student that the PBM Plan is going to help him say things like, "Now you listen and do what Mrs. Greene tells you to do; she is there to help you . . ." or "Now you tell her all your problems; she will take care of you . . ." or "Don't be afraid of Mrs. Greene; she won't hurt you." After any of these good-natured comments, what child could help but be terrorized? Sometimes it takes ten minutes just to calm the student down. If they are religious, they think I am a priest; whatever the relationship to their parents, I am like them; or maybe I am a psychiatrist, the family doctor or an Indian Medicine Man. One word from me and *presto*—they become perfect students. How frustrating!

These three are just some of the problems, but please understand that if you, as a PBM Administrator see a student, he must be receptive before you can initiate any program. The child must be working with you and feel that he has a vested interest in the outcome; you are not there to punish but to help. The child must understand your role as well as his, and you must begin on a footing that you *and* the child have built.

HOW TO USE FORMAL AND INFORMAL DATA

The type of information that a PBM Administrator uses falls into two categories, formal and informal data. Formal data consists of permanent record cards, health records, report cards, test scores and other standardized results. We use this type of information rarely simply because its very nature is abstract and cold; it gives facts about the child but very little sense of his personality. Informal data consists of teachers' reports, classroom observations, personal contact in more than one situation and compositions a child might write. This type of data provides a more accurate picture of the child in day-to-day situations, a picture never received from a permanent record card. I rely heavily upon this informal data, and I even consider the records I do keep in this category.

One of the requirements of the PBM Plan is confidentiality, and here the difference between formal and informal data is the strongest: formal data is *objective* and consequently, not open to interpretation. Anyone seeing or discussing the data must discuss abstracts of the child that do not break the bonds of confidentiality. Informal data is *subjective,* an interpretation of what is seen; even if based on some objective standards, it is primarily interpretation. The reasons for gathering informal data are limited, and the results should be equally as limited. The only people who should see or even hear of the cumulative interpretations are those directly related to the outcome. To all others, confidentiality must be maintained. Who should see the data? It varies: in one case, in order to help the child, his parents should be told; in another case it might be detrimental to do so. The discretionary power over this informal data must rest with the integrity of the PBM Administrator. If there is a doubt, all decisions must be reviewed by the building administrators.

Della told me in a Preventive Conference that she was toying with the idea of using marijuana. She said that one of her classmates (whom she named) was passing it out, and some of the kids had tried it. Now I had a problem: in order to get to the young pusher, I would have to tell someone; as soon as I did, however, I would break the confidentiality between Della and myself. After much agonizing, the problem went to the principal without any mention of Della, and it was handled in a discreet and satisfactory manner.

When we discussed the qualifications of the PBM Administrator in the last chapter, the three I's might have been included—Integrity, Intelligence and Ingenuity—integrity in knowing how to use formal and informal data and keeping all dealings in the PBM Plan confidential; intelligence, or common sense, in knowing when, where and how to handle a child's problem; and most important of all, ingenuity in solving interrelated problems in the simplest and most effective way possible.

But let's assume that the child is in the Program, the PBM Administrator is doing her job, and the child is beginning to change. There is a tool which can be used to reinforce the child's success and self-worth so completely that the change will be permanent: that tool is pride.

HOW TO BUILD PRIDE

There is something in the human being that wants to cry out even to the most casual onlooker, "I'm different; I'm somebody!" In the PBM Plan, we must recognize the need of self-worth in every child and reinforce self-worth at every opportunity. Sometimes this is not easy.

One way this can be accomplished is by a statement: "I know you can do it. 'They' don't think you can, but we'll show 'them'!" This formula of proof is what drives the students in PBM, for these students are different: for many reasons, they do not conform to the socially acceptable norms; they are constantly being singled out and set apart for negative reasons. They do not conduct themselves well in assemblies, so they cannot attend; they do not maintain themselves in class, so they must be removed; they can't keep up in their classes, so they must be given special attention or in extreme cases retained. They know they are different. The PBM Plan builds a *different* kind of difference. When everybody else has written them off, PBM stands by them and says, "How can 'they' think you're stupid? Just look what you can do! We'll prove it to them!"

The PBM Administrator must use this technique constantly. Every conference that the individual student has must build on past successes no matter how small. In each conference the PBM Administrator glorifies the individual's efforts. It is not unusual for me to tell a student having difficulties in several of his classes, "We've got 'them' on the run now; don't let up. Sooner or later 'they' will have to admit that 'they' were wrong about you!" Does this mean that I foster insurrection? No! I am using the power of the student's belief in himself and the fact that he can accomplish anything if he just perseveres. My belief in him becomes his belief in himself and a towering sense of self-worth.

There must be a second step. Singling out has always been done for negative reasons, and now the PBM Plan supplies a positive spotlight for the changed student. Someone even told me that after students are placed in the PBM Plan, they *look* different. They do! They walk differently, talk differently and act differently. They stand taller, seem happier, and act as if they are driven by an unseen force. The unobtainable becomes possible, they are unafraid to try anything and they begin to take education seriously. The school is theirs, and they begin to act *for it* with a vengeance. It is as if they are asking for a chance to prove not only that they are as good as the other students in the school, but that they are *better*.

We should give you a word of caution: do not feel that all of the students in the PBM Plan begin to glow with an inner light; they still have problems—some of them major. Now, however, instead of being against the school because the school was against them, they begin to look for ways to leave their mark positively. It is O.K. to get 100% on a spelling test or to have a teacher smile at you, but it's even better to have that teacher praise you or your efforts in front of the class. It is better if the principal praises your accomplishments and says they are good for the school. All students need to feel that what they do is important, and with the students in the PBM Plan this need is even greater. They have never been shown respect for any positive accomplishment. Once the student's growing sense of self-worth causes him to look for an outlet, the PBM must make an adjustment.

HOW TO ADJUST TO STUDENT GROWTH

How the PBM Plan in your school solves this problem is up to the talents of the PBM Administrator and the needs of the school. About two months into the Program, the problem of pent-up pride arose and I had to adjust the PBM to fill a supportive need. All of the tasks of the PBM Administrator are one-to-one. Was it now possible to put the individuals into a cohesive group without endangering their individual programs? I analyzed and analyzed the different kinds of problems the students in the PBM Plan had. At least three-quarters of them either had a basic disassociation with most of their peers or felt alienated from the educational system; they didn't seem to fit positively anywhere. The obvious solution was to have them do something to help the school that no other group was doing. Whatever the end result, the students in the PBM Plan had to claim it exclusively.

In every school there are certain clubs and activities that are exclusive. These always attract the elite. They are the very types of activities that the students in the PBM Plan equate with success but know they will never participate in. For example, the worst behavioral problem in the school never becomes the president of the student government; or the poor academic student never becomes the editor of the literary magazine. All expressions of pride usually are denied the PBM student due to his attitude, but now that attitude has changed. It would take too long for these students to go through the process of joining acceptable activities and bring their new-found patterns of success to light. There had to be another way.

When you decide to initiate this "self-worth reinforcement," here are some methods to adjust the PBM Plan to student growth:

1. The students must view the activity as something special to which they have never belonged; it must have prestige.
2. There must be a genuine need for the activity in the school; this is

not the time for a "busy work" activity. The results of the activity must make a difference in the school.

3. It must be physically possible; an automotive club in a school that doesn't have a garage is not possible. Also the culmination must be realistic. Even if it were physically possible to paint the school, it is unrealistic to assume that the activity would be permitted.

4. The PBM Administrator must propose the activity as if everyone thinks it is impossible *except* the PBM Administrator and the students in the Program. This is not the case since the building administrators must be consulted first, but the students must feel that their task is going to stand for something, namely, that they can do it.

5. Each individual must be made to feel that he has a part in the activity and that his effort is a requirement for its ultimate success or failure. Subsequently, when it succeeds he can rightfully claim credit.

6. Whatever the activity selected you, as PBM Administrator, must know how to run such an activity. If you know nothing about making a year book, don't decide to initiate the first one in your school's history.

Being aware of your students' needs will give you a rough idea of where they will fit in the organization of the activity. Some students may show leadership ability but have always used it in the wrong way; some students may have no desire to lead but need to belong to the whole; some students may have a particular talent which, because of their other difficulties, they have never expressed; and finally, some of the students may never have felt that their accomplishments would be noticed or approved by anyone in authority. Now, depending on the needs of your school, the talents of the PBM Administrator, and the students within the Program, choose an activity that will show off the students in the best possible way.

THE CASE OF THE FLAG'S FIRST EDITOR

I had reached the point described earlier where some sort of "pride builder" was needed for the students in the PBM Plan. Because I have some experience in journalism, and because the school never had a newspaper, I decided on that activity. I enlisted the aid of two teachers whom I shall call Mrs. Sperry and Ms. Mackie. These teachers had volunteered, and their help proved invaluable. We sat down one day and began to work out some of the procedures for implementing a school newspaper to be manned by PBM students. We knew that there would be difficulties ahead, but it was something that we felt had to be done; we were using the students that most others had given up for lost. To many, we were insane for even trying.

In all, 45 PBM students worked on *The Flag*, as the students finally named it. When Mrs. Sperry, Ms. Mackie, and I were in the planning stages we had to consider an editor. We knew exactly what this paper could be and could mean and almost simultaneously shouted the name of our editor, "Randy!"

Randy was different. At 13 he stood six foot two inches tall and weighed 273 well-muscled pounds. Through his background and his previous seven years of school experience he had "learned" that no one ever did anything for nothing; that no one was to be trusted because trust was a weapon they could turn on you; that any show of positive feelings was weakness that could destroy you; and that academic excellence was for "fags." Randy never joined anything, and his bitterness and barely hidden anger made him the most unacceptable student in school.

Randy's entrance into the PBM had been rather violent. He came into the PBM Room anxious to verbally assault and dominate this new adversary placed in his domain. When his, "Listen! I don't give a damn what you do to me!" elicited no response from me, he tried other attacks. Over the ensuing weeks he tried everything from a sullen, barely civil attitude to very sardonic, almost servile politeness.

When I told Randy that he was going to be editor, his comment was, "What do you get out of it?" We talked for a while and finally he declared that he would try it. We had to postpone the first meeting, however, since Randy was not in school because he had been picked up by the police the night before. Upon his return to school he was informed that he was still editor and had better get busy. He was amazed; he could not believe that I was not going to "throw him out."

That first meeting—five minutes into it I thought I was out of my mind. It was bedlam! They all got along with me, but not necessarily with each other. I tried to get attention but could not make myself heard over the din. Suddenly, out of the corner of my eye, I saw Randy get out of his chair and jump to the top of the nearest table. His "Shut the hell up!" almost broke the windows. In the stunned silence, I quickly got order and Randy returned to his seat.

Obviously there had to be some rules of order in the running of the newspaper meetings. They were, however, cautiously designed to reinforce acceptable behavior of the school. In the silence that followed Randy's outburst, I outlined the plans for the paper, spelled out the rules and gave the reasons for each. One rule was no leaning back in the chairs. I no sooner said this when Randy rather noisily leaned back in his; he was sure of his dominance over the other staff members, and now he was going to prove his dominance over me.

"O.K., Randy, please put your chair down."

Randy complied until I looked away, and then the chair went back on two legs.

"Randy, put the chair down."

This time the chair stayed on two legs. Randy, with his legs straight out and his arms crossed against his chest, grinned at me.

"Randy, if you don't put the chair down I'm going to dump you on the floor."

Randy stayed where he was.

"O.K.!" I bent down, grabbed the two legs of the chair and dumped him. Slowly, Randy rose from the floor, stood six inches from me, glared down at me, and started to laugh.

"Damn, you really did it!"

"That's right," I said. "Now sit in the chair. I don't say things I don't mean."

The staff started to laugh, and almost in one motion

Randy and I turned and glared them to silence. The struggle for power was over, and both Randy and I had won: he would comply.

Posters had to be put up advertising the first issue. We tried to get them all up before the end of the school day, but there were still many rooms that had not received theirs. Rather than wait until the next day, it was suggested that we hang them as a surprise when the teachers and students came in the following morning.

Gathering up posters, thumbtacks, masking tape, etc., Randy started out the door. Realizing that some rooms might be locked, I flipped Randy the master key to the school, asked if he needed help, and asked him to get back as soon as he could since there were other things to do. Several moments after he left, it dawned on me what I had done: I had sent out Randy, a person who had shown no regard for other people's property and whose spitefulness could turn a disliked teacher's classroom into a shambles, with a key that opened every lock in the school!

I panicked—do I run after him? Send another student on the pretext of helping? Do I wait for the reports of stolen articles the next day? While there had been some improvement in Randy's behavior, I had no doubt that he could revert to his old patterns at any time.

About twenty minutes later Randy walked back into the room without the posters, flipping the key. He walked directly to my desk and, almost gently, set the key before me. I looked up to find him staring directly at me. For the first time since I had known him and in a barely audible voice he said, "Thanks—thanks a lot."

The day the paper came out, the enthusiasm the student body showed was overwhelming. We had sent an advance copy to the Board of Education, and a letter of praise from them combined with official praise from the school administration made it a perfect day. Randy could not contain himself. At the end of the day I was coming out of my room when Randy, halfway down the hall, spotted me. "Mrs. Mamchak!" he shouted. "We did it! We did it! Damn, this is really something else!"

Randy was never the same again. Never an honor student, with a mouth that was too careless and too fast, he had started to trust, and began to believe that doing something good was not a sign of weakness. He learned that he could get people to do things without bullying them. Perhaps most importantly, he came to believe that there really were people who wanted to help him with no ulterior motive.

As far as I was concerned, *The Flag* and its first editor were both successes!

10

How Administrators and Teachers Can Use the PBM Plan

The only ideas that *work* for us are the ones we put to use. The PBM Plan is a viable, working program, and there is something in it for you.

Figure 10-1 will give you an idea of where the PBM Plan fits within the structure of the modern school. Its parallel standing with faculty and specialists makes it easily supervised by administrators and yet readily accessible to all aspects of the school, especially the students. It can and should be utilized by everyone.

HOW TO INCREASE YOUR ADMINISTRATIVE EFFECTIVENESS

As an administrator your day begins five minutes before you are ready for it and ends an hour after you thought it had. Quite often it is nothing but a series of interruptions; there is just so much to do.

With the PBM Plan there is a way to structure at least one of your priorities, namely the need for immediate, consistent and fair discipline.

Let's take Johnny who has just been removed from Mr. Mann's class. The why's and wherefore's of course are important, but by the time you sort it out, you will miss that meeting of fifth-grade teachers you faithfully promised to attend.

With the PBM Plan, you send Johnny to the PBM Room and know that shortly you will receive the precise information

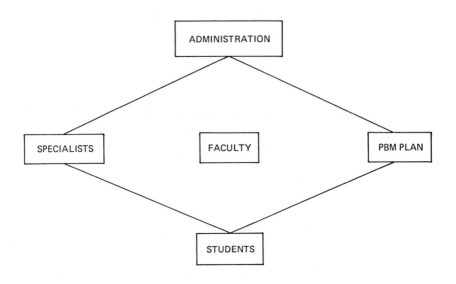

THE PBM PLAN WITHIN THE SCHOOL STRUCTURE

FIGURE 10-1

to enable you to settle the matter equitably. There is little interruption of Johnny's education and no missed meeting.

You also can use the PBM Plan to achieve a more positive image among the student body. Like it or not, your role is viewed by many students as the "rebuking parent" or the omnipresent, omnipotent authority. But you know that the punitive role is only one that you play; you are also the "approving parent" when you watch an assembly, or an "information giver" when you enter a classroom. Under the PBM Plan these positive roles increasingly become the primary reason for student contact. Consider the power for positive action you will have with the student body behind you.

How often have you picked up the phone to tell a parent that her child has misbehaved? Conversely, how often have you been called with the question, "How is my child doing?" Unless the student is a severe discipline problem or is exceptionally bright, you may have to think a moment to recall that child to mind. The PBM Plan will not help you to remember the names and academic profiles of 700 students, but it will give you more opportunities to call parents for positive reasons and a greater insight into their child's educational progress.

Let's take an actual example. Mrs. Jay calls you concerning her sixth-grade daughter's difficulties in math; she is quite upset. When the PBM Plan is in your school, you can tell Mrs. Jay that you will place Mary in the program, and that you are sure that she will see results very soon. You contact Mary's math teacher and recommend placement in the Academic Achievement Factor. A week later, after viewing the PBM weekly abstract, you call Mrs. Jay and relay some positive results. Your image with the parent is now one of actively working for her child's good. Keep that up, and you may find the school budget passing.

The longer the PBM Plan is in operation in your school, the more you as an administrator will find uses for it. It will ease your busy schedule, help you achieve better enforcement of "rules and regulations" with greater justice, improve your image among the student body, and aid you in involving parents in positive ways. It is ideally suited to your needs.

GUIDELINES FOR REALIZING YOUR FULL POTENTIAL AS A TEACHER

The disruptive student is always of concern. There is a time element involved inasmuch as the time spent controlling the disruptor is learning time taken away from the rest of the class and the disruptor himself. Yet he must be handled before he causes further disruption. Now you are faced with a dilemma: you wish to keep him in the learning environment, but if you do the rest of your class will suffer. If you remove him, you have solved your problem, but not his. How to continue the learning process while disciplining the student is what is handled by the Referral Factor of the PBM Plan.

What's happening to Billy? He was a friendly, affable,

helpful child on Monday, and in the space of two days has turned into a bully. You can see that if this continues, Billy may be headed for very serious difficulties. With the PBM Plan functioning in your school, you can contact the PBM Administrator, relay your observations and concerns, and request that Billy be seen. Look at the advantages: Billy's behavior comes under immediate scrutiny by a person who is concerned, but divorced from his day-to-day experience—much like the child who told me he had "wet the bed" the night before but couldn't tell his teacher because then she would always know that he was a "bedwetter!" Whether it is as light as this or of a more serious nature, the point is that you, the teacher, can get help in pinpointing the problem *before* it becomes a problem, and in such a manner that there is no punishment associated with it.

While the Teacher-Requested Conference can be used for behavioral changes, it can also be used to channel a student into the Academic Achievement Factor. As we have seen, this assistance is at your direction and is a reinforcement of your teaching methods.

Finally, the PBM Plan weekly abstracts can be made available to teachers of students involved in the Program. By using these abstracts you can see the progress of the individual student and deal with him more effectively on an individual basis.

STRATEGIES FOR INCREASING SPECIALISTS' PRODUCTIVITY

The most attractive feature of the PBM Plan for school specialists (school psychologist, social worker, nurse, learning disabilities specialist, guidance counselor) is the ability it provides them to use their student contact time most productively.

The PBM Administrator at no time replaces or supersedes any of the specialists; his or her function is to observe, report, aid, follow through and report again. Let us look at how each specialist can use this unique procedure.

A whole week to store up problems for one day—this is a

description a school psychologist gave me on how her role was viewed by many of the schools she serviced. On a given day she has between ten and twenty-five students to see, as well as innumerable teacher, parent and administrative conferences. Occasionally, psychological testing is added to the day's schedule. The picture is staggering!

Let's add the PBM Plan. The anecdotal studies completed by the PBM Administrator can serve as helpful background material for new referrals to the psychologist. Once the child is seen, the PBM Administrator can follow progress and under specific direction can report any deviations immediately. This "leg work" enables the school psychologist to "zero in" on specific areas of concern.

A social worker can use the PBM Plan as another resource when handling particular problems because the anecdotal records show the students' attitudes within a specific period.

Marty always shows up in the nurse's office just as second-period geography starts. There are no identifiable symptoms, but the child still appears. The nurse knows that the child isn't ill but can't and won't prevent him from coming. You can use the PBM Plan to find the underlying cause of the "flight" to the nurse's office.

Throughout this chapter the use of patterns and resources has been emphasized. No one uses these more effectively than the guidance counselor or schedule coordinator. The PBM Plan illuminates some underlying reasons for student misconduct, and this information can be used to circumvent future difficulties.

Take Sammy, for example: Sammy was scheduled into a classroom where the structure was very free and open. Sammy did not perform well in this environment; he excelled only when the work schedule was structured and he had limited choices of actions. If a choice next year were between another open classroom and a more traditional one, his guidance counselor would have Sammy's results to ponder. It should be noted here that there is no reference to personality clashes or student misconduct nor should there be, for these can be overcome. The basic work environment is the concern.

Figure 10-2 illustrates the basic structure of the PBM Plan. Notice that the PBM Administrator is in contact with specialists, parents and the students; consequently, the PBM Administrator is in an excellent position to be of service to all.

Specialists are in school to aid the educational process. Heavy work loads, increased enrollment, and changing laws do not make their jobs any easier. Teachers, knowing their students need the attention of the specialists, are impatient with delays. The PBM Plan makes data available to the specialists, which increases their ability to handle more students more effectively and to return their valuable opinions to teachers in time for them to help the students.

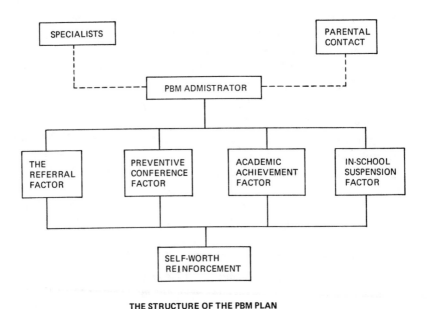

THE STRUCTURE OF THE PBM PLAN

FIGURE 10-2

HOW TO PROMOTE STUDENT GROWTH EFFECTIVELY

In your classroom you are trying to aid the student's growth in skills, knowledge and experience. Each day you are faced with the challenge of how to do this effectively. The PBM Plan is practical and productive only if students can use it; there is no magic involved. It is a studied, precise outgrowth of what you yourself do in every class period. How does a student use it? It is not a weapon; it is rather like an encyclopedia to which he can go for information and further reinforcement. The student's reliance on his own actions leads to greater harmony within your class, but more importantly, within the student himself. As it gives him a feeling that he is part of the school, he loses the sense of "me against them." Many times students have told me that the Plan makes them feel they are not alone.

You are concerned that Alice is upset and cannot concentrate. The PBM Administrator may find that Alice has just broken up with her first boy friend. It's a big problem to Alice, but certainly in relationship to her productivity in your class, it is a greater one. When Alice discusses her problem with the PBM Administrator and is given tools for handling the situation, her problem is put in perspective, and your class continues smoothly.

Once a child is in the program and the PBM Plan has helped in one situation, there can be applications in similar situations. Because the program enforces socially acceptable behavior, students begin to verbalize anger instead of letting it out physically, eventually averting the situation entirely. They begin to rely on authority rather than taking matters into their own hands. Instead of making excuses for their actions, they begin to see that they cause what happens to them and consequently, they must face the reality that *they* must change. The teacher's benefit here is outstanding: the student is constantly told and shown that you are there to assist him, and as he begins to realize and believe this, you begin to grow in his eyes.

HOW TO DETERMINE WHEN YOU CAN UTILIZE THE PBM PLAN

We have discussed the general uses of the PBM Plan on all levels. Now let's take a look at *your* school. Take a moment and answer, honestly now, these 14 questions:

1. Is there a student in your class whose behavior has drastically changed within the last month?
2. Do you have a student whose behavior has caused you to call his parents, keep him after school, or send him out of class?
3. Has one of your students begun to fall behind in one or more subjects?
4. Have you been waiting for a report on a child whom you referred to one of the specialists?
5. Do you have a student who is perfect for you in the morning but "rotten" for you in the afternoon?
6. Are you confused by one of your "darlings" being called a monster by another teacher?
7. Do you have a student who, while normally very good, today was a terror?
8. Can you see the need for a room where one of your students could quietly study a specific subject for a specified time with supervised assistance?
9. Could you use help with one of your students who is having difficulty with his peers?
10. Would you like a "third opinion" during parental conferences?
11. Would you like the ability to ascertain "guilt" before "sentencing"?
12. Do you have a problem in your school such as vandalism, false fire alarms, fire crackers—that you have been unable to contain?
13. Are there students in your school who are chronically truant?
14. Are you seeking an alternative to out-of-school suspension?

Did you answer more than eight of these questions "yes"? Then you most assuredly can use the PBM Plan. It is a source of information when you have a question, another option when you are seeking an alternative, and a tool when you have a specific task to handle.

KEY STEPS TO RELYING ON THE PBM PLAN

Let us assume that now the PBM Plan is in your school. Administrators—you now have no need to make snap decisions; the PBM Plan gives you the chance to get the facts to ponder before your decision. Let it work for you; once you have set the procedure, stick with it. It is consistent. Teachers—it is a tool for your use. Let it work for *you*. Communication is a two-way tool; if you want to know something—ask. Your problems can run the gamut from student attendance to the slow learner. With the PBM Plan, the flow of information is continuous; in fact, the more demands you place upon the PBM Plan, the more it can help you. The PBM Plan, however, can only do what you ask of it; the PBM Administrator initiates nothing. No one knows the problems you have but you. So share them.

I was sitting in the teacher's room one afternoon. Beside me were two teachers discussing a student. Both were complaining that they didn't know what to do and that the problem was driving them to distraction. Suddenly, one of them turned to me:

"Just you wait," he told me jokingly, "sooner or later, you'll get him!"

I asked what the problem was, and both teachers gave me their observations.

"Why don't you send him to me now?" I asked them. "I'll see what I can do for him. Why wait until he gets into trouble? Let's see if we can prevent that."

Both teachers expressed surprise since they didn't think that I would take a child *before* he had caused some difficulty. The teachers involved had considered only the Referral Factor of the PBM; they had neglected to consider the Preventive Conference Factor which aims at containing a problem before it *becomes* a problem.

The point is that once the student's difficulty is out in the open, the PBM Plan can go to work. If the PBM Administrator does not know that a problem or even a potential problem exists, then nothing can be done. Remember that teacher's room complaints will not solve problems—use your new tool.

One of the procedures of the PBM Plan is the involvement of parents. This certainly can work to your benefit. Surely you must have seen the amazement that comes over some parents when you tell them that their child is misbehaving. They look at you in a bewildered manner and reply, "My child??? Oh, it's not possible!"

Actually, it *is* your word against theirs. There are many cases where a child is polite and well behaved at home but becomes "Mr. Hyde" the moment he or she passes through the doors of the school. Under conditions such as these, can you blame a parent for doubting you?

Now let's assume that the PBM Plan is in your school. If the child has been in difficulty, PBM has already involved the parents in the child's progress. Now at the time of a conference, the parents are fully aware of what has transpired; more importantly, however, you are no longer looking at the student's problems from opposite sides. Now, because of the positive involvement that the PBM Plan sponsors, you and the parents are a team working *together* toward a single goal. This cooperation between home and school is a powerful instrument in aiding the child.

Moreover, in the case of an uncooperative or antagonistic parent (few and far between; most parents with whom I come in contact are most cooperative), the PBM Administrator may be called in for a report or to reinforce previous discussions. As you will see in the next chapter, PBM has methods for ensuring positive parental involvement, and these methods are at your disposal.

Once one of your students has been placed in the PBM Plan, other uses will occur to you. Remember, the PBM Plan takes its direction from you. The punitive role in the Plan is constantly played down; and *nowhere* is this better understood than in the classroom. The student is referred to the PBM Room for noncompliance with your rules or directions. In the PBM Room he is given the tools and incentive to comply; back in the classroom, his efforts are "rewarded" with your approval. That's not punitive action—that's a learning process.

One final word: sometimes teachers or administrators may be reluctant to refer a child or a problem to the PBM. Why? Perhaps they feel that to do so is to admit that they can no longer handle the problem themselves, that the plan is a usurpation of their authority, or that "giving up" is a sign of weakness. To feel this way is to misconstrue the basic purpose of the PBM Plan: the PBM Plan is in the school as an aid to the teacher, administrator and specialist. A doctor may consult with other doctors on a particular diagnosis, but the patient is still his. A lawyer may consult with other lawyers about a particular legal difficulty of his client, but it is still his client. When you rely on the PBM Plan, it is to handle a specific problem, but the jurisdiction is still yours.

The PBM Plan is in your school to help *you.* Use it!

11

Techniques for Involving Parents

It has been stated earlier that one of the serious difficulties with the current options for handling student behavioral problems is their reliance upon parental authority. The PBM Plan also needs parental involvement in many cases. This is not a reversal of opinion, however, for the PBM Plan takes a different approach to the parent's role. Instead of relying upon parental authority, the PBM Plan requests parental responsibility.

THE TEACHER'S GUIDE FOR UTILIZING THE PBM PLAN WHEN DEALING WITH PARENTS

Never have I seen such furious activity in a school than just before Parent Conference Week, probably quite similar to preparations for the advancing armies of Attila the Hun! Let's make sure that all the failing papers are on record so the disgruntled parent won't be able to threaten to get the mark changed and the teacher fired for incompetence. Let's hear those familiar grumbles about the only parents they would probably see were the ones they didn't need to see, and why didn't Mrs. X come in so she could see what a problem her child really was?

Humorous? On the contrary—how terribly *sad*. Instead of preparing for short up-dating and informational meetings between educational partners, the teachers view this precious time as a battleground for adversaries.

Within the PBM Plan, involvement with parents is ongoing. It is not something to be confined to certain weeks, or the ends of marking periods, or incidents of violent misbehavior. Everyone benefits from this, especially the teachers. Communication is opened with parents the teachers have never met before. In some cases, the parents are more "turned off" to school than their children. When parents become involved, the teachers find that their seeming unwillingness to take an active role in their children's education is nothing more than a defense against something they do not understand, a feeling of being unwanted and a fear that someone may doubt their ability to control their own children. Once the hand of friendship and cooperation is extended to these parents, most of them are willing to do almost anything to help.

You may say, "But, I've tried everything . . ." This may well be true, but hasn't there always been that string attached? The "string" is the teacher telling the parent what must be done, and usually at unrelated times and in situations where the parent's protective instincts produce a barrier. Using the PBM Plan, however, teachers are in contact with parents for such a myriad of reasons that no connotation of disapproval can be sensed by the parents involved *or their peers.*

This last statement is not as far-fetched as it sounds. My mother was leary of going to school because of what the neighbors might think. One mother whose son was involved in the PBM Plan could not drive and was transported by her sister-in-law; any drive to school always produced a comparison of the sister-in-law's children to hers. In order to avoid this, the PBM mother did not attend school functions or teacher conferences for four years!

And even if they do come in, parents as a rule are seldom asked their opinion; after all, teachers are supposed to know how to handle children. In some cases this thought becomes so ingrained in parents that if something does go wrong in the school, their reaction is, "That's your problem; you handle it!"

Yet it need not be like this. Let's look at a situation in which a teacher utilizing the PBM Plan destroyed the barriers and built firm lines of cooperation with parents.

Mr. Wilson became concerned that Jerry could not seem to pass his English tests with marks commensurate with his abilities shown in class. Jerry always did his homework and participated well in class discussions. Mr. Wilson contacted the PBM Administrator and received a report that Jerry felt he just "choked up" on tests; the PBM Administrator further suggested that Jerry's parents should be contacted. The next day Jerry's parents met Mr. Wilson and immediately started complaining bitterly about how unreasonable it was that their child's entire mark depended upon passing one test.

Mr. Wilson was amazed. Where did they get such an idea? Why from Jerry, of course; in fact, Jerry became so upset before the test, they reported that he was physically ill.

Mr. Wilson fully explained his marking system and showed how Jerry obviously had misunderstood.

Now that they understood the problem, Jerry's parents suggested that they would explain this to their son and would help him study for all future tests. The problem no longer existed once both sides had met and communicated openly.

The keys to the teacher's use of parental contact within the PBM are as follows:

1. Enlist parents' aid; don't condemn them.
2. Compromise for the child's best interest.
3. Remember that it is cooperation rather than control by either party that will aid in the educational success of the child.

PBM GUIDELINES FOR DEALING WITH PARENTS

As shown in Figure 10-2, the PBM Administrator draws upon the parents for much needed information and assistance. Just as vision problems should be reviewed with the nurse, behavioral problems should be reviewed with parents. It goes without saying that there are times when this parental contact must be handled very delicately. The first concern of the PBM Administrator must be the rapport and confidentiality established with the student; involving the parents must not supersede this priority. The child must accept his parents' involvement, and in most cases this can be accomplished merely with an explanation of the Administrator's intent. There is, however, a guarantee that you will never divulge anything to the parent that the child does not wish divulged. The role of confidentiality must also be extended to cover the parent: if the parent honestly believes that the child's problem is one of his teachers, then this must be investigated honestly. There are personality clashes between parents and teachers, and these too must be dealt with calmly, and subsequent information must go no further.

The main reason for involving parents in the PBM Plan is to increase the understanding of their role in the educational growth of their child.

HOW TO ESTABLISH RAPPORT WITH PARENTS

Extending a friendly hand isn't going to turn a reluctant parent into a PTA president all by itself. This first gesture is like a bone offered to a strange dog: no matter how good it is, it must be sniffed and examined first. Keeping this in mind, make the first contact as light and nonthreatening as possible.

I once contacted a parent to find out whether a class project the student said he left at home indeed was left there. When the mother picked up the phone I said, "Hi, I'm Sue Mamchak from _____ School . . ." That is as far as I got. She proceeded to tell me that her son had stayed up until 2 a.m. and if he was in trouble, it was my fault because he was tired.

"Whoa, slow, I'm not Jimmy's teacher. I'm merely trying to find out if you need any help transporting his project to school this afternoon. I just met Jimmy. He's involved in a new program, and I thought if he needed help, I'd find out from you." This was all said very quickly, for I could sense she either was going to hang up the phone or blast me again. Instead I got silence, followed by, "What's the new program?" I briefly explained that it was a program to help her son in school.

"Oh! Well, his project is sitting on the dining room table. I don't know why he didn't take it. He was so tired this morning, he didn't even eat breakfast!" This began another shorter tirade on why schools keep children up until 2 a.m.; there was no point in discussing the matter further, so I asked again if she needed help getting Jimmy's project to school.

The story continues, but I wish to point out two things that I did *not* do: first, I didn't tell her I was checking up on her son or doubting his honesty; and second, I didn't become involved personally in her anger over her son staying up so late.

After the first contact, efforts should be made to establish a personal, friendly relationship with the parent. At first, your professional role with the school is played down to the parents. They must feel that they have free access to the program and that you will act on their behalf for the best interest of their child.

There is a bit of manipulation here: your intent when contacting parents is to make them aware of their parental responsibilities, but they must discover these responsibilities themselves. A friendly suggestion or hint from the PBM Administrator will aid in this discovery process. If the guidance is too light, the parents might not develop that sense of responsibility; if it is too heavy, they may feel manipulated and their resentment toward the school may become even stronger. Establishing rapport first eases the flow of information and assistance between home and school.

DEVICES FOR DIRECT PARENTAL INVOLVEMENT

There are two methods of communication in the PBM Plan, verbal and written. I find that in the beginning, particularly for the first contact, verbal communication is best. Since this usually takes place over the telephone, careful attention should be paid to inflection and statements in order to insure parental involvement. As soon as it seems reasonable, I follow up the conversation with a letter, which I discovered has two benefits: first, to the parents it immediately destroys the old idea that a letter from school means trouble; secondly, to the child it reduces the fear that when his teachers and parents get together he is in trouble.

Repeatedly, the PBM Plan tries to destroy stereotyped thinking at whatever level it might exist. Children's attitudes toward teachers as well as teacher's attitudes toward chronically disruptive students obviously must be changed if they are so prejudicial that they impede educational growth. Parental prejudice is also a great factor in shaping some student's attitudes; in these cases, the parents must change before their children can. Direct involvement must be real. The parents must be given tangible and positive things to do; they must become actively involved in the school's effort to aid their child.

Consider this analogy: suppose you were going to see an actress in a movie and you know she always plays the part of a shrew. You take all the publicity about her, add it to her current role and you have a preconceived notion of what she must be like: *you don't like her!* Now suppose that actress moves into your neighborhood. You begin to see her in the supermarket, at the gas station, in the library; and to your surprise, she's just like normal people! She has become involved in the community, she knows the postman and the merchants, she knows the layout of the streets and who lives in which houses. She's O.K.

Many parents have a preconceived notion of school, all teachers, all principals and educational concepts in general; they are outsiders. The PBM Plan brings them in, and they begin to see the real school. They see day-to-day education, not as dramatic perhaps as a graduation or Parent's Day, but much more realistic. They know what the bells mean, who teaches in that classroom, and what it is like in the halls when the classes change. To do this, obviously, the PBM Administrator must get the parent physically into the school.

So there are three steps to direct parental involvement; each one must be a smooth and logical outgrowth of the other: first, establish verbal, friendly rapport, usually by phone. This leads to the second step of calm, informative written communication. The third step is to bring the PBM Plan and the parent face-to-face, the inference being that letters still allow for the kind of byplay that parents prefer. It becomes logical for parents to come to school. They know why they are coming; they come with a task to do, with information to give, and a stake in the outcome. With that combination, you can't lose. You are not meeting with an enemy but with an interested, active participant!

A UNIQUE METHOD FOR INSURING
POSITIVE PARENTAL INVOLVEMENT

One of the qualifications of the PBM Administrator is the ability to communicate with individuals of all ages at all levels. The involvement of the parent shows how valuable this asset is to the PBM. The Administrator's objective is to get the parents to make the same suggestion that he wanted to make all along, but to make them feel it is their idea. When this happens, the teacher can act upon it positively; and the parent feels accepted, feels less defensive toward the school, and begins to help the child in those areas which the school cannot.

Sound confusing? It really isn't. The objective has always been there, but the stumbling block is the method. Using the three steps outlined, try some of these methods:

1. *Verbal*

   a. "I'm having a problem understanding a situation that arose in school . . ." This method shows a willingness to listen to a parent's appraisal of a situation.
   b. "I wonder if you could help me untangle an argument . . ." This method tells a parent that something has happened but you are willing to seek their information before making any decisions.
   c. "Your child told me you might help me . . ." Regardless of what the situation may be, the parent won't let her child down.
   d. "I wonder if I might be of assistance . . ." This is the method used in the example of Jimmy's class project. It assumes that the parent might not be aware that a problem is developing.

All of these verbal methods are worded to elicit positive responses, to avoid any defensive attitudes and to encourage rapport.

2. Written

a. "I'd like to bring you up to date..." This assumes a relationship that is ongoing and needs their involvement.
b. "The situation is progressing, but..." Involvement is on-going, but you are seeking input from them for a specific situation.
c. "Progress has been noted, and the results are now evi-dent..." One situation has now been handled, and they can take part credit.
d. "We solved... is there anything else..." Once the parent is involved, this insures future involvement.
e. "I wish you could see..." or "Perhaps if you saw..." This is the logical introduction to them coming to school.

Several letters should be exchanged in order that this line of communication assumes a positive rather than a negative connotation.

3. Physical, In-school

a. "How nice to see you..." or "Want a cup of coffee..." or "Would you like to go to the teacher's room or my room..." Common sense dictates that a "guest" be treated cordially upon arrival. Your first meeting with a parent should follow convention.
b. "I spoke with... would you care now to go over..." Getting to the business at hand gives purpose to the meeting.
c. "Walk with me so that you can see..." Physically walking a parent around the school serves a two-fold purpose: 1) first-hand knowledge of physical environment; 2) their presence is not something secret, but their prerogative.
d. "While you are here, is there anything..." This method

assumes that their positive involvement may be needed in
other areas.
e. "I hope I see you ... how about next ..." Communication
is now open, accessibility shown, and an assumption made
that they will return.

These methods have the cumulative effect that parents
become familiar with the school; they are there for supportive
purposes, and their positive involvement is both sought and
appreciated.

Methods of involving parents positively all assume that the
parent wants to be involved. Unfortunately, there is a very small
percentage that feels parental responsibility stops on the first
day of school; they will never be reached. Between these two
extremes, however, lies the "hostile parent."

HOW TO DEAL WITH THE HOSTILE PARENT

Let us first define what we call the "hostile" or "syndrome" parent. It is not the normal "personality clash" that most
teachers might use as a definition. This parent, usually reluctant, can be positively involved using the methods described
above. The hostile-syndrome parent, on the other hand, cannot
be reached even with these unique methods; he or she is
"hostile"—characteristic of an enemy; unfriendly or antagonistic. These parents view the school as a very real enemy in a
continuing battle which they must wage to protect their child.
The parents who fit this definition have many specialists upon
whom they can draw for reasons why their child behaves the
way he does. The testimony of these specialists is seemingly
irrefutable by the school or the classroom teacher.

A hostile-syndrome parent must contend with one or more
of the following:

1. A child with a borderline, diagnosable and *controlled* physical
impairment (symptomatic asthma, epilepsy, diabetes, etc.).
2. A child who is physically handicapped but has been *trained*
(canadian crutches, hearing aid, etc.).

3. A child with a previously diagnosed, *now controlled* emotional problem (stuttering, mildly hyperactive, etc.).
4. A home environment in which a sibling is emotionally or physically handicapped.
5. A home environment that is filled with discord (violent arguments, "missing" parent, etc.).
6. A personal environment where one or both parents either have an emotional or a physical handicap.

The outward sign of the hostile-syndrome parent is either condescending ("Of course you don't understand, perhaps you would like to contact Dr. A..."), informative ("Dr. B will handle..."), accusative ("How can you do that to my child? Don't you know that he's..."), or apologetic ("My child cannot be expected to ... Don't you know that he is...").

The school must deal with the children who fall into these categories since they are indeed capable of being mainstreamed. Those incapable are in special classes, but the students with whom PBM deals *are* in the general student body and are subject to all of its rights, privileges *and* responsibilities. When one of these students gets into difficulty, some parents fall back on the problem that exists, rather than facing the child's present difficulties. The hostile-syndrome parent at best is protective of what he or she feels is a weakness, and at worst is infuriated and uses the child's disability as an excuse for any misconduct.

The PBM Plan is invaluable in working with this type of parent, for even where it does not solve all problems, it opens avenues for discussion previously unmentionable. Some methods in this area are as follows:

1. Reading up on the child's difficulties so they can be discussed knowledgeably with the parents. Certainly, this does not make one an expert, but it prevents the off-hand tossing of medical jargon so that the child's present problem can be discussed.
2. Thoroughly reading the student's health records so the parent realizes you do have a background knowledge of the child. This usually involves discussions with other school specialists.
3. Controlling your own personal feelings and, at least at first, doing what the parent demands. If a mother wants Dr. A contacted,

contact Dr. A; but this is only at the beginning. Then bring the parent back to the present situation under discussion.

Obviously, common sense and the PBM principles mentioned earlier will be of use in continuing relationships. Just remember that the way to handle a hostile-syndrome parent, one who displays the "characteristic of an enemy," is to show the characteristics of a friend, be empathetic and focus the lines of communication from defensive to positive involvement. The rewards are boundless.

"MEET THE PARENTS"—THREE CASE HISTORIES

One of the nicest things about writing a book is the right to put nice people into it. These three people are just such people. Each in her own way showed what can (and did) happen when parents are actively and positively involved with the school through the PBM Plan.

Mrs. Marcia Carpenter is the mother of Cliff, a rather high-strung sixth-grader. She had been active in the PTA throughout her child's school life and knew most of the teachers in the building. They were familiar with her, and they generally called her the "nice parent." When Cliff was placed in the PBM, there was no difficulty in getting him to allow me to involve his mother. Everything was fine, right? What need was there for the techniques of the PBM? Just a major one: I asked her what she thought could be done to improve Cliff's production of homework, and she was stunned. No one had ever asked *her* opinion before! Up until now, the teacher had told her what to do, and she went along. Working together as equal partners, Mrs. Carpenter, the teacher and I began working out a program to help Cliff. When he began to improve, both she and Cliff felt rewarded. This warm, calm, genuinely interested parent had now found a way to be actively, positively involved in her child's education.

Mrs. Jean Nichols' child, Ann, had been in trouble almost from her first day in school. She had heard every tirade, plea and approach the school could give her. After five years of this,

Mrs. Nichols developed strong defensive attitudes, and when I approached her, she was ready to take me on. Using the techniques of the PBM Plan, Jean and I quickly established a working rapport, the major outcome of which was helping Ann overcome a negative outlook toward school partly developed by her mother. Ann's progress was slow but steady, and Mrs. Nichols became an actively involved parent.

And finally, there is Mrs. Rose Morely. I must smile to myself as I think of this hostile-syndrome parent. Her son, Scott, was a chronic classroom disruptor. In the third grade he had psychological testing that showed him to be over-reactive and mildly hyperactive. A mild sedative was prescribed after Scott had undergone closer psychological observation. Off and on over the next four years, Scott came under psychological review with the medication lessened or strengthened depending on test results. All observations concurred, however, that Scott was quite capable of handling a regular classroom situation. Soon after the PBM Plan was instituted in the school, Scott was sent to me. The next day I received my first phone call from Mrs. Morely. Finding no satisfaction in talking to me on the phone, she demanded to see me. Our first conference consisted mainly of a step-by-step description of her son's psyche coupled with comments about what a nasty, deplorable, unfeeling so-and-so I was to pick on her poor son. I had done my homework well, and I asked her questions like what strength valium he was taking, and had the doctor ever prescribed librium? In the midst of her speech, she stopped in utter amazement. She threw a doctor's name at me, and before she could go on I asked if she would like me to talk to him. Naturally, it took many discussions with both Rose and Scott before any progress could be clearly seen, but what a joy of understanding we experienced as the three of us opened lines of communication between ourselves and then the school at large.

When teachers use the PBM Plan to involve parents directly in positive participation in their children's development, the chances of a child's success are vastly improved. When the child succeeds, in a very real way you and the parents have succeeded as well.

12

The PBM Administrator's Guide to Successful Record Keeping

This chapter and the one that follows are companions: The "you" in this chapter is the PBM Administrator, while the "you" in Chapter 13 is the experienced educator within the school. Each comes to the PBM with a different perspective but with equal needs for practicality. Here, then, is the efficient backbone of the functioning PBM Plan from the PBM Administrator's viewpoint.

WHY RECORDS ARE NECESSARY

For the efficient functioning of any system guidelines or records must be kept. For the PBM Plan, however, this is not merely for efficiency, but for productivity and success as well. Without accurate records the patterns of behavior might go unnoticed, the nuances of changing behavior might go unseen, the times for release could be misjudged, and communication could lose the sharp accuracy needed. These are the real PBM reasons for keeping records. Naturally, records make the PBM Administrator's day-to-day job easier, but more importantly, they make the PBM Program more effective.

A FEW TIPS ON ACCURATE RECORD KEEPING

Among the requirements for the physical setup of the PBM Room, there is a file cabinet, a typewriter, and some form of communication. Following some basic guidelines, let us see what each one does.

First, the file cabinet . . . here are kept the manilla file folders on each student. They are divided into those students who are actively engaged in the program, those who have been released, and those who have left the building (through graduation or transfer).

In this setup, the file cabinet becomes the physical housing for all the student data in the PBM Plan. A three-drawer method seems to work best: the top drawer is for actives, the second drawer for inactives, and the third drawer for those students no longer in the building. When one of my students is about to be released, I explain this system and then move his file from the top drawer to the second as a further physical reinforcement of his progress. This action never fails to be greeted by a wide smile.

Now for the typewriter . . . If your handwriting is like mine, you *need* a typewriter; and no matter how poor your spelling may be, the typewriter is at least clear and legible.

My typewriter has a companion, a Rolodex (R) flat file. This holder of 3 x 5 cards proved so invaluable that Dexter, as I call mine, is helping us write this book. In the main files are the complete explanations of all the meetings, but it takes only a few seconds to jot down a few pertinent facts on a 3 x 5 card and file it in Dexter. Later, a flip of my fingers gives me whatever information I want. While the files in the cabinet might be seen by someone, Dexter and I are secret.

Finally, the communications system . . . With the file cabinet and a flat file (or Rolodex), abstracts can be written; once written, they must be dispersed. Records kept for communication (memos, abstracts, evaluation reports, etc.) must be clear and concise, yet if they are accessible to students, they must be somewhat guarded. Dependent upon how your communications system works, checklist or paragraph type forms may be used.

There are a few more suggestions which you may find helpful in your day-to-day record keeping:

1. Keep your records brief; if one or two words bring an entire incident to mind, use them. If you feel that you may lose the meaning, however, schedule time to elaborate.
2. Where possible, use checklist type forms; these are easy to fill out and easily read. Teachers particularly do not wish to be encumbered with forms that waste precious classroom time.
3. Where possible, write down exactly what the child says, trying to capture inflections as well as words.
4. Go through your records periodically and condense any small pieces into easily read abstracts. For example, you will begin receiving communications from parents. By the end of several months, you may have six or seven letters from one parent on file. At this point, it is better to pull the letters, abstract the contents and unless particularly important, discard the originals. Teachers' reports also may lose importance with time. Condensing them makes the files easier to manage and easier to read.
5. One last tip: don't keep things in your head! If you schedule a student for a conference, write it down; even if the student remembers, you may well forget. If you tell a teacher that you will look into something, make a note of it; the teacher will come to you two days later wanting to know the results. Six months into the Program you may be dealing with the schedules, patterns of behavior and their changes, of as many as 130 students. Above all, the PBM Administrator must have a precise knowledge of dates and commitments. Effective record keeping is how you remain efficient.

THE FIVE PBM FORMS

There are five major PBM forms. There are also two additionals, three abstract structures, and one grid. These are all the data-seeking or data-giving forms of the PBM Plan.

The five major forms are as follows:

1. The Administrative Discipline Report Sheet (Figure 12-1)—This comes from the office.
2. Referral Sheet for Disciplinary Action (Figure 12-2)—This is used by the PBM Administrator and can be adapted to an Academic Referral.

3. Conference Report (Figure 12-3)—This is used by the PBM Administrator and/or teachers.
4. Student Progress Report Sheet (Figure 12-4)—This is used by teachers and parents.
5. Conference Pass (Figure 12-5)—This is used at all levels.

The two additionals are as follows:

1. Student Evaluation Sheet (Figure 6-1)
2. Student Schedule Form (Figure 7-2)—Further use of this form as a record-keeping device is shown in Figure 12-6.

The three abstract structures are:

1. Teacher Report Sheet (Figure 12-7)
2. Weekly Abstract—Sent to the administration.
3. Bi-Monthly Abstract—Sent to the administration.

Finally, there is the grid as shown in Figure 4-1.

HOW TO USE THE PBM FORMS

The following step-by-step procedures are practical outgrowths of my handling of situations.

Step 1
The student enters the room with the Administrative Discipline Report Sheet (Figure 12-1). After reading it, pick up the Referral Sheet for Disciplinary Action (Figure 12-2).

Step 2
Transfer all pertinent data where called for and begin the conference, mentally using the grid (Figure 4-1). The Referral Sheet enables you to make an anecdotal record as the student speaks. This raw data will never be seen, but it will assist greatly in analyzing the student later.

Step 3
Fill out a file card on the student and place it in the table file. This should be done on the typewriter, while the

ADMINISTRATIVE DISCIPLINE
REPORT SHEET

Student's Name:_____ Date:_____

Teacher: _____ Grade: _____

REASON FOR REFERRAL:

ACTION PREVIOUSLY TAKEN:

_____
_____

ACTION TAKEN:

COMMENTS:

FIGURE 12-1

ADMINISTRATIVE DISCIPLINE
REPORT SHEET

Student's Name: _Brad Howell_   Date: _10/17_
Teacher: _G. F. Singer_   Grade: _4_

REASON FOR REFERRAL:

Fighting in class – abusive language – generally disruptive!

ACTION PREVIOUSLY TAKEN:

Brad has been repeatedly warned about his behavior. This is merely another incident in a long chain of disruptive acts!

ACTION TAKEN:

Sent to Mrs. Mamchak for remainder of day.

_M. G._

COMMENTS:

FIGURE 12-1

155

**REFERRAL SHEET FOR
DISCIPLINARY ACTION**

Student's Name:_____ Grade:_____

Homeroom:_____ Date: _____ Time: _____

Referred By: _____

REASON FOR REFERRAL:

COMMENTS (HOW STUDENT VIEWS HIS/HER REFERRAL, PAST DATA ON STUDENT, AND OBSERVATIONS):

RECOMMENDATIONS:

FIGURE 12-2

REFERRAL SHEET FOR
DISCIPLINARY ACTION

Student's Name: _BRAd Howell_   Grade: _4_

Homeroom: _K. Kole_   Date: _10/17_   Time: _11:37_

Referred By: _G.F. Singer_

REASON FOR REFERRAL:

    Fighting in class - abusive language - generally disruptive.

COMMENTS (HOW STUDENT VIEWS HIS/HER REFERRAL, PAST DATA ON STUDENT, AND OBSERVATIONS):

    "I hit Billy - Singer got all upset" Attitude was shown thru smirks, shrugging shoulders, etc. when asked to describe incident, he spoke in term of others - not his actions.

    I have never met Brad before, but have seen him causing disturbances in the hall. I have told him he will be placed in the program - "Big Deal" was his reply.

RECOMMENDATIONS:

    I will go thru the usual procedures with him. Will see Brad on Thursday 10/19.

                                _P.S.M._

FIGURE 12-2

157

CONFERENCE REPORT

_____
(Date)

_____   _____
(Name of Student)   (Homeroom)

WORK HABITS: *(Circle the one that applies.)*

EXCELLENT   GOOD   SATISFACTORY   FAIR   POOR

BEHIND, OR NOT DOING WELL, IN_____

_____

GENERAL COMMENTS ON WORK HABITS _____

_____

_____

BEHAVIOR: *(Circle the one that applies.)*

EXCELLENT   GOOD   SATISFACTORY   FAIR   POOR

SEEMS TO HAVE DIFFICULTY WITH _____

_____

GENERAL COMMENTS ON BEHAVIOR _____

_____

_____

RECOMMENDATIONS:

FIGURE 12-3

158

CONFERENCE REPORT

10/18
(Date)

Brad Howell   106 - K. Kole
(Name of Student)   (Homeroom)

WORK HABITS: *(Circle the one that applies.)*

EXCELLENT   GOOD   SATISFACTORY   FAIR   (POOR)

BEHIND, OR NOT DOING WELL, IN *almost all subjects except Science.*

GENERAL COMMENTS ON WORK HABITS *Brad will only work on whatever interests him! Very little, poorly done homework! Wastes time!*

BEHAVIOR: *(Circle the one that applies.)*

EXCELLENT   GOOD   SATISFACTORY   FAIR   (POOR)

SEEMS TO HAVE DIFFICULTY WITH *interpersonal and peer relationships!*

GENERAL COMMENTS ON BEHAVIOR *Easily excited! Great difficulty with peers! Picks on classmates! Resents any correction!*

RECOMMENDATIONS:

Try to straighten this one out! He's got the potential if only he can learn to control himself.

G. F. Singer

FIGURE 12-3

159

PROGRESS REPORT SHEET FOR THE WEEK ENDING _____

Teachers:

　Below you will find a copy of _____'s weekly schedule.
It is divided into sections for your convenience. Opposite the subject you teach you will see a space
space for comments on _____'s progress last week. If the work has been satisfactory,
just put a check mark in the space provided. If not, then comment as to why it has not. Finally,
please initial your entry.

　Beneath the schedule, you will see that there is a space provided. If you feel _____ needs
further help in any area, please use this space.

SUBJECT	COMMENTS	SATISFACTORY	INITIALS

FURTHER COMMENTS:

FIGURE 12-4

STUDENT PROGRESS REPORT SHEET FOR THE WEEK ENDING *10/27*

Teachers:

   Below you will find a copy of   *Brad Howell*   's weekly schedule.
It is divided into sections for your convenience. Opposite the subject you teach you will see a space
space for comments on *Brad*   's progress last week. If the work has been satisfactory,
just put a check mark in the space provided. If not, then comment as to why it has not. Finally,
please initial your entry.

   Beneath the schedule, you will see that there is a space provided. If you feel *Brad* needs
further help in any area, please use this space.

SUBJECT	COMMENTS	SATISFACTORY	INITIALS
English	Brad's work in my subject		K. K.
Speech	still leaves a great deal to		
History	be desired. A small amount		
Civics	of progress has been shown.		
Creat. Writ.	He handed in homework		
etc.	2 out of 5 times.		
Math	Somewhat better!		G. F. S.
Gym	Misbehaves in class!		HLR
HEALTH	No Homework this week.		UE
Sci.	Fair!		K.J.
Music	Very disruptive!		tt

FURTHER COMMENTS:

   art - Very poor!   *JR.*

FIGURE 12-4

161

CONFERENCE PASS

_____ IS REQUIRED TO SEE ME FOR A CONFERENCE
          (Name of Student)

AT_____ ON_____
      (Time)   (Date)

IF ABSENT, PLEASE NOTIFY ME BEFORE CONFERENCE TIME INDICATED.

THANK YOU.

TIME LEFT CLASS: _____

TIME LEFT CONFERENCE:_____

FIGURE 12-5

- -

DATE: _____

Dear_____,

This is to inform you that _____ will not be present in

the following classes. Please initial and return.

1.				
2.				
3.				
4.				
5.				
6.				
7.				

If there are any questions, please state them on the back of this sheet. Thank you.

FIGURE 12-6

CONFERENCE PASS

Brad Howell   IS REQUIRED TO SEE ME FOR A CONFERENCE
(Name of Student)

AT___*10:30*___ON___*10/19*___
   (Time)   (Date)

IF ABSENT, PLEASE NOTIFY ME BEFORE CONFERENCE TIME INDICATED.

THANK YOU.

TIME LEFT CLASS: ___10.27 *Q5.*___
TIME LEFT CONFERENCE: *10.43 P.M.*

FIGURE 12-5

DATE: *1st Semester*

Dear *Brad Howell*,

This is to inform you that *Weekly Schedule* will not be present in the following classes. Please initial and return.

	MON.	TUES.	WEDS.	THURS.	FRI.
1.	MUSIC-TIMMONS	HISTORY-KOLE	CREATIVE WRITING - KOLE	ART-PERRINE	SPEECH-KOLE
2.	ENG.-KOLE	ENG.-KOLE	ENG.-KOLE	HISTORY-KOLE	ENG.-KOLE
3.	GEOG.-KOLE	GEOG.-KOLE	CIVICS-KOLE	CIVICS-KOLE	HISTORY-KOLE
4.	MATH-SINGER	MATH-SINGER	MATH-SINGER	MATH-SINGER	MATH-SINGER
5.	SCI.-JATON	SCI.-JATON	SCI.-JATON	SCI.-JATON	SCI.-JATON
6.	GYM-ROBERTS	HEALTH-COX	GYM-ROBERTS	HEALTH-COX	GYM-ROBERTS
7.	HISTORY-KOLE	READING-BARR	READING-BARR	READING-BARR	READING-BARR

If there are any questions, please state them on the back of this sheet. Thank you.

FIGURE 12-6

TEACHER REPORT SHEET

DATE: _____

TO: _____

FROM: P. S. MAMCHAK

RE: _____

FIGURE 12-7

TEACHER REPORT SHEET

DATE: _10/18_

TO: _G.F. Singer_

FROM: P.S. MAMCHAK

RE: _Brad Howell_

George,

    I have spoken to Brad about both his work and behavior. I am convinced he feels he can get away with almost anything. I have hopes of changing this.

    I will be seeing Brad Thursday mornings (much as I did with John). He knows he must complete all work + maintain good behavior until conference.

    If there is anything else you would like, please let me know.

                  P.S.M.

FIGURE 12-7

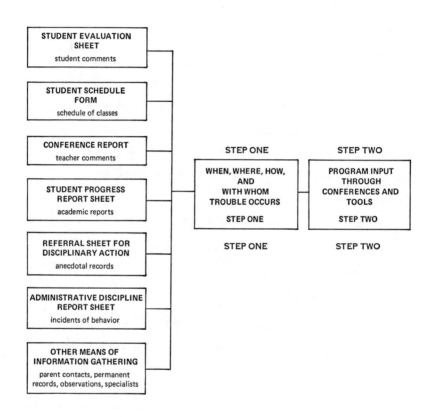

FIGURE 12-8

STEP THREE

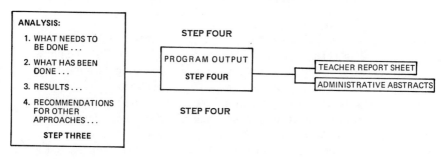

ANALYSIS:

1. WHAT NEEDS TO
   BE DONE ...

2. WHAT HAS BEEN
   DONE ...

3. RESULTS ...

4. RECOMMENDATIONS
   FOR OTHER
   APPROACHES ...

STEP THREE

STEP FOUR

PROGRAM OUTPUT

STEP FOUR

TEACHER REPORT SHEET

ADMINISTRATIVE ABSTRACTS

STEP FOUR

STEP THREE

FIGURE 12-8 *(cont.)*

anecdotal record may be done in longhand (carefully). Be sure to comment in the "Recommendations" section, as it will assist you in setting up a Conference Schedule.

Step 4

If the student is to remain in the PBM Room, use the Student Schedule Form (Figures 7-1 and 7-2) as explained on pages 93-96.

Step 5

Whether or not the student is to continue in the PBM Room, within the next two days send a Conference Report to the teachers involved (Figure 12-3). This form has multiple uses: in one instance it can be an information gatherer; in another instance it may be initiated by the teacher as a request for a conference; and later on it may be used as a short progress evaluation report for a conference.

Step 6

If the student is going to be seen again, the Conference Pass (Figure 12-5) is filled out and held by the PBM Administrator. It is then delivered to the teacher during the homeroom period of the appointed day. This form also has other uses: to a student with a chronic problem, the Conference Pass can be used by either him or the teacher to gain immediate access to the PBM Room. At this point, a Student Schedule Form can be reused as seen in Figure 12-6. Once the student fills out a weekly schedule, you have another tool for both scheduling and analysis.

Step 7

Within four days, the teacher should receive an abstract on the Teacher Report Sheet (Figure 12-7). If the student is to remain in the program, these abstracts are sent upon the teacher's request or at least once a week.

Step 8

By whatever communication system seems the most appropriate, once a week a Student Progress Report Sheet (Figure 12-4) is circulated among the teachers involved. This is used as an information gatherer for both an input for analysis and an output for administrative abstracts.

Step 9

As the student progresses toward the successful conclusion of his PBM Program, the Student Evaluation Sheet (Figure 6-1) is used as discussed on page 85.

As you become familiar with each one of the forms, you will see that they form a cohesive block of informative data, each form with its own purpose, but all aiming toward pinpointing with precision the student's difficulties, progress and success. Now let's see how we can analyze these records.

A STEP-BY-STEP GUIDE FOR ANALYZING RECORDS

When you have used your forms, you now have a series of pieces which can be fitted together to show an accurate picture of the student. It shows when, where, how and with whom the difficulty usually occurs. Look at the graphic portrayal of this in Figure 12-8. Assuming that you have completed this first step, Step 2 is the PBM input which has been discussed throughout the book. Step 3 is the review and the analysis. Let's take an example.

Brad, the student in the figure examples, has gone through the procedures of Referral. The PBM Administrator begins a file; after a series of conferences, information has been gathered (gets in trouble in gym, doesn't do homework, fights with Billy) and the PBM Administrator encourages the use of tools for change (Step 2). At this point one or more of the factors of analysis (Step 3) is possible. Going through these steps several times will help to pinpoint the analysis. Finally, the PBM Administrator must abstract the analysis in such a way that evaluation is possible. Figure 12-8 should make this clear.

HOW TO PREPARE ABSTRACTS TO AID
THE CLASSROOM TEACHER

When filling out the Teacher Report Sheet (Figure 12-7), the PBM Administrator must be informative, concise, and must give the classroom teacher a clear understanding of what PBM is doing with the particular student. The bonds of confidentiality must not be broken in this information technique. Read Figure 12-7 carefully, and you will note that at no time is the substance of the conference revealed, yet the teacher has a firm understanding of what will be done. The recommendation of setting up a Conference Schedule is made, and the teacher's comments and cooperation are encouraged. Always be sure that the abstracts can be used by the classroom teacher as an extension of normal teaching methods. For example, to recommend that the child be seated on the floor is neither usual in a class nor likely to conform with the teacher's management techniques. Furthermore, the teacher confronted you with a problem and expects you to devise a solution. Be decisive in your recommendations without being demanding. Finally, the teacher wants to know if you basically agree that there is a problem. Your analysis after meeting the student should mention some of your observations and what you might consider to be the major problem.

The PBM Plan is basically a tool to aid the classroom teacher in reducing the loss of educational time from student behavioral problems. The abstracts are your methods of communicating your solutions and assistance.

HOW TO USE YOUR ABSTRACTS
FOR GREATER COMMUNICATION

We have seen how the use of abstracts leads to clear understanding between the PBM Plan and the classroom teacher. Other lines of communication, however, are equally important. The use of administrative weekly and bi-monthly abstracts is a vital step in this communication process. Communications *is* understanding. The more understanding of how the PBM Plan aids the school, the less problems the PBM will encounter. It has been demonstrated, for example, that there is no relinquishing of power by the administration. By way of proof, the administrative abstracts are the PBM Administrator's soliciting of aid from the administration.

There are two types of abstracts, each serving a different purpose:

Type 1: Weekly Administrative Abstract

The purposes of this abstract are to list the students seen, show why they were seen, briefly update data if they were previously in the Program, and in some cases pass on for consideration an analysis for possible recommendation.

An example of this type of abstract follows:

Student Referrals:
a. Bill Michaels—disrupting class in which a sub was present. This is Bill's first referral this year; he was sent twice last year.
b. Henry Allen—creating problems for both himself and his teachers. The idea of him reporting to me between home-room and class somewhat backfired. Since we must be aware of where he is at all times, and since Henry must take some responsibility for his actions, I will give him the daily pass you suggested he carry. He will pick up a new one each morning from his homeroom teacher and return it to me each night before going home. Is there any other method you feel would accomplish this better? I will do as you recommend.

A comment on this: while the PBM Administrator can initiate conferences and conference schedules, it is necessary that this should be known by the administration. Methodology is a negotiable point, but the building administration must know what is going on. Their responsibility for what happens in the school gives them final approval for any changes in the course of a PBM Program which might not conform to their guidelines.

Type 2: Bi-Monthly Administrative Abstracts

The purpose of this type of abstract is to break down the PBM Plan for administrative analysis. It lists the data by grades, homerooms and types of PBM involvement. It summarizes the statistics of the PBM Plan clearly for review.

An example of this type of abstract follows:

IV. Summary

Certain facts have become apparent: first, 63.9% of the problem students handled within the Program last year have not been in difficulty in the first two months of this year. Second, of the 31 active students, nine (29.1%) are new to the Program. Finally, these "new" students are concentrated: five in the seventh grade, two in the eighth, and one each in the fifth and sixth.

Another comment here: in a very real sense, the continuation of the PBM Plan can rest upon the precision of these bi-monthly abstracts. Aside from personal contacts with you and comments from the teachers, the abstracts are the only tangible evidence of the progress fostered by the PBM Plan within the framework of the school.

When these two abstracts are used to their best advantages, the PBM Administrator and the building administration can develop the open lines of communication so necessary to them both.

In many lines of work, record keeping may be viewed as just a tedious task of compiling useless data that no one will ever see, much less use. The PBM Program, however, actively uses every piece of data collected and passes on vital information and suggestions to those eagerly waiting to use this new tool for increasing students' educational success. The task is made efficient by the concise forms and the results are dynamic communication.

Evaluating the PBM Plan

You, the experienced educator, are well aware that evaluation of any project is both necessary and proper. Whenever something new is tried, evaluation reports are usually required at all levels from school boards to state Departments of Education. Monies have been expended, and results must be shown. There is little value, however, in a "paper success."

Of course, you know what a "paper success" is: our schools are littered with them—new programs or new ideas whose objectives are so worded that when the project is completed whatever results are listed can be "fit in" to meet these loosely phrased objectives, and the whole program can be shown as a grand success. This technique, while certainly not illegal, seems to indicate that the project cannot stand on its own.

There is no opportunity for equivocation in evaluating the PBM Plan. Following the procedures explained, you will discover that evaluation boils down to PBM either doing or not doing what it says it does.

AN ADMINISTRATIVE GUIDE FOR PROJECTING RESULTS

Perhaps when you began to understand the limitations of your present options and began looking for new methods of coping with student behavioral problems, you thought that the PBM Plan was that long sought-after method. Whatever your reason, whether it was the claim of less suspended students, more parental involvement, less repetition of disturbances, or whatever, *that* was your reason for trying the PBM Plan. *That* is what you wanted it to do. The pilot phase of a program usually lasts a year. You know what you want from the PBM Plan, so projecting results can only be done in terms of whether or not there is a successful completion or attainment of *your* goal in *your* school.

Let us take some of the goals just mentioned: you want more parental involvement. Did you get it? The PBM Plan claims to lower suspensions. Were they lowered? Again, the evaluation of the PBM Plan must be done in terms of *your* expectations.

You have received from the PBM Administrator the bi-monthly abstracts which show how the students in your school are being processed through the PBM Plan. These abstracts show the types of offenses and the ways they are being handled; weekly abstracts are used to show the individual progress of specific students. Your suggestions and recommendations have been sought and acted upon throughout the pilot year, and you have a stake in the outcome. When projecting the results, you have to ask yourself if your efforts have been rewarded. Is the PBM Plan making your administrative job easier? Is educational time being used more productively than before? Instead of evaluation being a passive, equivocating arrangement of results to fit open objectives, have you taken an active role along clearly defined goals toward a concrete conclusion of success or failure? If the program is working properly in your school, you need not wait till the end of the year—you know long before that. Your teachers, too, have been actively involved in evaluating the PBM Plan.

A TEACHER'S GUIDE FOR PROJECTING RESULTS

In one of the schools with which I was involved, a group of teachers had started work on an inter-disciplinary program involving block time, correlated curricula, outside resources and a wide panoply of instructional methodology. Upon the completion of their first year, they were asked to compile an evaluation *booklet.* I worked with them closely, and although I noticed that the required evaluation was rather petty (among other things they wanted to know was how much time was spent going to and from the lavatory), they were able to comply because of the work they had done before the project started. Each one of the group knew both long-range and short-term objectives. When the reading level before and after the project was requested, the statistics took time, but were done because the objective of advanced reading levels was proposed from the beginning.

The PBM Plan has no booklet for you to fill out, nor should it have. It is our sincere hope that by now you, the classroom teacher, can see that the PBM Plan is designed to help you. The objectives of PBM closely parallel the behavioral objectives you have set for your own classes. The evaluation of the PBM Plan should be based on this one question—did it help you?

One of the ways in which the PBM Plan is practical is by setting realistic goals. For example, the PBM Plan will *reduce* incidents of vandalism in the school. To say that *no* window will ever be broken, *no* book will ever be torn, or *no* wall ever written upon is relating a dream and not a practical objective. Certainly you as a teacher must project results depending upon what the PBM Plan states it will do for you. Last year you had to replace 25 textbooks because they were covered with obscenities, ripped and torn, or otherwise generally abused. This year, with the PBM Plan in your school, you had to replace only ten. Has vandalism in your class been reduced?

The PBM Plan claims that there will be more positive parental involvement. Last year, parent conferences were a shambles: there were misunderstandings, breakdowns in communication and even a few overtly hostile reactions. This year the parents you saw were mostly helpful; in difficult cases, the PBM Administrator was there to help. Suggestions rather than demands were made by both sides and you found that you and the parents were talking about how best to aid the child, not about personalities. Has there been more positive parental involvement since the advent of the PBM Plan in your school?

If your answers are affirmative, then the PBM Plan has delivered what it claims. The next thing you have to decide is whether or not the plan should be continued.

A CHECKLIST FOR THE CONTINUATION OF THE PLAN

Once you have decided upon your objectives and the Program has entered the pilot phase, approach the question of whether the successful attainment of the objectives warrants the continuation of the Program. Let's be practical for a moment. If the PBM Plan doesn't make dynamic changes in your school, why keep it? If it is not helping your students, faculty and administration, why go through the trouble of even having it in your school?

From my administration of the program, I prepared a rather lengthy list of objectives with companion evaluation questions. Below is an excerpt taken from that checklist. Please note that there are allowances made for both objective and subjective evaluations:

1. How many students were actively engaged in the program?
2. How many classroom disruptions were handled?
3. How many students were released from the PBM Program?
4. How many students had to be removed from class more than once? More than twice? Three or more times?
5. How much time did you spend in handling punitive contacts as compared to last year? Was it more, less or about the same?
6. Was there a difference in parental contacts?
7. How much money was spent replacing vandalized materials? Was the amount higher or lower than last year?
8. Were there attitudinal changes in your school? Were they for the better?
9. Were there more group projects involving large numbers of students?
10. Were there extracurricular activities opened to include the previously unmotivated student?
11. How many students were processed by the school psychologist this year? Last year?

12. How many schedule changes had to be made this year as compared to last year?

In light of these questions and others like them, an evaluation of the PBM Plan can certainly be made and even statistical data established. In retrospect, it is possible to determine what it was like and what it is now. On the basis of this data you should have a firm foundation for determining whether or not to continue the PBM Plan in your particular school.

One of the questions for evaluation should involve attitudinal changes in the school. This is something that the PBM Plan does sponsor, and the proper interpretation of these changing attitudes is essential to understanding and evaluating this aspect of PBM.

HOW TO INTERPRET CHANGES IN ATTITUDES IN YOUR SCHOOL

Short of listing every attitude that existed in your school both before and after the initiation of the PBM Plan, your interpretation of changing attitudes in your school must be subjective. There are, however, some useful guidelines.

Let us assume that one of the attitudinal difficulties in your school involves a changing nationality grouping in one of the school's contributing districts. Suppose one group claimed that all the "bad things" that happened in the school were done by the "usurpers." You are well aware that the attitude of hostility and prejudice inherent in this situation could keep your school in a constant turmoil. Given these conditions, even a subtle shift toward the fact that students are no longer antagonistic *for the same reason* is a change for the better. John does not like Luis because Luis ripped up his paper, not because Luis is Hispanic. That is a change that is possible under the PBM Plan.

Let's take another attitudinal change. The same child might well change from, "Why should I go to school? It don't teach me nothing!" to "If I read this here book, will it tell me

why a airplane don't fall down?" The grammar remains as bad
in both statements, but something very positive has been added
to the second question. Inquisitiveness and the added positive
reinforcement of the PBM Plan can change an attitude for the
better.

Changes in attitude seem subtle only because they take
place over a long period of time. It is a basic assumption of PBM
that certain attitudes will change. Parents will become more
personally involved with the school; students will become more
anxious to learn; and stereotyped thinking will be changed.
These attitudinal changes are long-term goals, but they are built
on the foundation of piece-by-piece, short-term successes. One
of the things that we discovered is that success in one area
usually brings success in other areas as well. It may sound
strange, but once the PBM Administrator shows a student how
to work successfully in English, the child sometimes becomes
more willing to change his attitudes toward a minority, or
toward teachers, or toward authority in general; and with the
proper guidance and reinforcement from PBM, he does so.

Obviously, this area of evaluation is subjective. This does
not make it invalid; it merely means that you must be
open-minded and fair. If you think your school has changed for
the better, fine; if you think it is the same, say so. If, however,
you are satisfied that attitudes have changed but you want the
attitudes to change *even further,* then you should state them as
your objectives for next year, not as a failure this year.

HOW TO DETERMINE HOW FAR YOU HAVE COME

The title for this section is from a question on an
evaluation sheet issued by an educational consulting firm. We
took particular notice of it because it made us angry since it
assumes that some kind of utopia is going to exist at some point
down the road. You know better! You and the PBM Plan
decided to join forces to solve specific problems. After working
together for even a short period, you began to find that the
initial problems were being solved and others were beginning to

take their place. The PBM Plan does not offer any utopia; in fact, it will be forever finding places where it can aid you. Once it has handled one problem, you can turn it to work on another.

This means that evaluations must be precise; those completed at the end of a PBM year are vitally important, for they show the direction in which you are going next year. Remember, there is no place in PBM for a "cosmetic" evaluation. The PBM Plan doesn't have to be made to "look good" for anyone. No extravagant claims were made for it, and no extravagant, hyperbolized evaluations are needed either. Don't alter or exaggerate anything—let the results speak for themselves.

Evaluations should not be regarded as tests, but rather as sources of information. They can tell you what has been done, what areas require greater effort and they can show you how specific techniques were or were not received, etc. There is no end to the information you can derive from a good evaluation. Why should anyone consider it a test? The implication of a test is that there are right and wrong answers. This is absurd! Think of it rather in terms of a map which you are using to find various routes to help you arrive at solutions to problems.

When you are deciding to continue a program, certain factors must be taken into account (how much money is available, subjective liking or disliking of the program, availability of space and personnel, etc.). An evaluation already assumes that you are going to continue—why else would you be so specific in wanting to know how the techniques work? If you have to justify canceling a program, you can do it for any number of reasons that do not need specific data. Evaluations are working tools for a working program.

TIPS FOR EVALUATING STATISTICAL DATA

Benjamin Disraeli, the 19th-century statesman and Prime Minister of England, once claimed that there were three kinds of falsehoods: "lies, damned lies, and statistics!" This statement contains more than a grain of truth: in our own experience we all can find instances where some clever individual manipulated statistical figures to prove almost anything. Advertising does it all the time to sell everything from toothpaste to automobiles. Does this mean that you can't use statistical data when endeavoring to evaluate the PBM Plan? Of course not, but statistical data should be used as illustrations and not as proofs.

As illustrations, statistics can show you the rise and fall in specific types of behavior during specific periods of time, the numbers of students seen during those same periods, etc. These are objective pieces of data. When you use statistics to prove subjective statements, however, you can fall into the trap of distortion.

I discovered the truth of that last statement through bitter experience. When it came to the point where I had to evaluate the PBM Plan that I was administering, I included statistical data. The following are two statements from my own records regarding the PBM Plan:

1. 84% of the students I saw were not referred to the Program for a second behavioral problem.
2. 69.7% of the students I saw never got into behavioral difficulty again.

Both of the above statements are accurate; that is to say, both events took place. One statement, however, is objectively accurate, while the other is statistically disputable—which one was arrived at by statistical manipulation?

If you answered statement number two, you are right. What I meant to say was that after going through the program and being released, 30.3% of the students I saw re-entered the Program; they came back a second time. However, I was evaluating the Program; I was equivocating, and I wanted it to be a positive statistic rather than a negative one.

Perhaps my intentions were indeed "honorable," but the statistic is misleading. I admit it. That is why it is particularly important to be careful when using statistics.

If, however, the method to be used is primarily statistical, then some guidelines for their preparation are necessary. Here are a few ideas that I find helpful:

1. Make sure the statistics are objective.
2. Use one set of statistics for each point (by linking statistics false assumptions can be made).
3. Keep comparative statistics to a minimum. Showing that apples are like oranges cannot be objective once the subject of fruit has been left behind.
4. Do not use statistics to expand a theory to a generalization or to condense a generalization to a specific. Here again statistics should be illustrations and not proofs.
5. Full explanations of all data must be given *before* the mathematics. Statistics in and of themselves are not explanations.
6. Do not distort statistics with loaded words or phrases. If the math works out to 38.6%, saying "almost half" is extremely misleading if not absolutely false.
7. The converse statistic may not be true or accurate, as shown in the example given in the text.

The use of these suggestions will make your job somewhat easier and, hopefully, will make your statistics practical. Not to offer practical solutions is at best misleading and at worst a lie.

There are three phrases in this chapter that may cause some concern—paper successes, cosmetic evaluations, and statistical manipulation. There may be well-founded reasons for each one, but they are extremely harmful to the educational process.

Moreover, there is no need for them in the PBM Plan. What need is there for a paper success when the objectives have been clearly obtained? What need is there for cosmetic evaluation when the school is actively benefiting from a program? What need is there for statistical manipulation when simple subtraction or division of objective figures readily demonstrates success of the Plan?

In short, how do you evaluate the PBM Plan? Simple. Did it accomplish what it set out to accomplish? No? Then discard it! Yes? Then you have picked a winner. Stick with it!

14

How to Effectively Overcome
Problems that Affect the PBM Plan

Any time you work closely with individuals and establish interpersonal relationships, there are bound to be problem areas. Recognizing these problems is not the admission of a flaw but an understanding of their existence. To recognize that a problem exists is the first step toward its solution. None of the problems facing the PBM Plan are debilitating, but they must be dealt with effectively.

"WHERE'S JOHNNY"—A GUIDE TO
ESTABLISHING COMMUNICATION

As stated earlier, one of the greatest strengths of the PBM Plan is its accessibility. Students can feel free to come to the PBM Room. There could be an underlying problem in this, however, if it were taken to its logical conclusion: children might be running in and out of their classrooms all through the school day. Teachers might not know where members of their classes are; and a point of friction, while annoying in the beginning, might build to a resentment that would destroy the Program. Furthermore, some students could use this accessibility as an excuse to get out of tests or disliked class periods, or to avoid some impending punishment. The tightrope here is much the same as that used by the school nurse, described earlier: while the nurse neither could nor would ever turn a child away, some regard must be taken for the general running of the school.

Teachers must be made aware of students who have been placed in the PBM Room. Let us assume that a teacher is taking roll, finds a student missing and marks him absent. Unless met by a chorus of yells from her class, "Johnny was kicked out of Mr. Ames' class!" the teacher may not know where her student is.

Of all the communication problems encountered in other programs, this is the one that the PBM Plan tries the hardest to overcome. With the Plan, there is very little loss of educational time; with the use of some communication tools, there will be no "loss" of students either.

There are several ways to overcome this particular problem. The first is to institute the use of two forms, the Conference Pass and the Schedule Form. The Conference Pass (Figure 12-5) allows teachers to know immediately how long a child is going to be out of class. Since the passes are signed and timed, aimless walking in the halls and class cutting is avoided. Conferences are scheduled in such a way that students are not always pulled from the same classes. Moreover, alternate times can be arranged for those cases when a conference is inconvenient due to a classroom activity. Even though the PBM Administrator must be able to hold conferences, the teachers can easily communicate their desires and arrange changes.

The second form, the Student Schedule Form (Figures 7-1 and 7-2) is used as explained on pages 93-96. This is particularly successful in eliminating the problem usually encountered when a child is removed from class. By circulating the form, gathering classroom assignments, and turning in a student's completed work, the teachers are made to feel that the student is still a part of their class. They still exercised control over the assignments and work produced while the PBM Plan is handling the behavioral aspects of the situation. Teachers must have this control; without it an estrangement grows between the student and his class which hampers a smooth re-entry after the incident.

All too often the teachers do not know what is happening to their students once they leave the class. The PBM Administrator works diligently to keep open the lines of communication. Rather than, "Out of sight, out of mind," the child is passed from hand to hand with careful guidance and certain knowledge on the part of all concerned.

HOW TO LISTEN INSTEAD OF JUST HEARING

No matter how well structured lines of communication may be, there are still times when what is said is not what is meant. A prime example of this is a student who angrily yelled at his teacher, "Go ahead and send me to Mrs. Mamchak—I'd rather be there than here!" Granted, the situation is fraught with emotion; but if you could listen, that is pay attention to what was meant, the student might have been saying anything from, "I've got to get out of here," to, "Can't you see I've got to save face?" It is important that you do not misinterpret what the student says, and it is equally important that you under-stand what he means as well. I find that when some students speak to me, particularly the ones I get to know well, the meaning of what they say is much more important than the words.

As you know, children in elementary school range in age from six to fourteen. Let's deal with the little ones first. They have the greatest imaginations in the world. They are not lies, mind you, merely their side of the story. If you believe everything a seven-year-old tells you, particularly in situations of stress, you might begin to think that his mother really would execute him on the spot for losing a pen! Isn't the child really saying, "I'm scared!" or, "My Mom is going to be mad at me!" even if he isn't saying it out loud? For students a little older, I use the wording on the grid (Figure 4-1). Indeed, I took the advantage out of lying, but that didn't prevent some students from taking a chance on it every now and then.

If you start to listen instead of just hearing, you should be aware of a problem that may develop. The persons selected as PBM Administrators must be able to empathize: they must be warm, outgoing and sensitive; as much as possible, they must remain detached and not personally involved. However, this is easier said than done. Of the students with whom I worked, four or five of them "got to me." I knew it was happening, but there wasn't much I could or would do about it. Yes, dependency is a problem, and to be perfectly frank, I think it is unavoidable. To a very few, the PBM Administrator *will* be the mother, sister or friend they desperately need. PBM Administrators must cope with it as best they can, be aware of it, and try not to let it get out of hand. If they cannot control it, they should bring it up with the building administrator. Dependency is not a destructive force if it is occasional; it only becomes a severe problem if too many students fall into the category. The main goal of the PBM Plan is for students to gain self-reliance and to internalize socially acceptable behavioral patterns. If the students are only working to please the PBM Administrator or because they have a strong emotional attachment and dependency upon the PBM Administrator, then the whole character of the PBM Plan has changed. When the goal becomes, "You must please the PBM Administrator," the program is in trouble.

HOW TO DEAL EFFECTIVELY WITH MISUNDERSTANDING

Misunderstanding can come from two basic sources: lack of knowledge or the misuse of knowledge. Proper communication can help, but there are times when misunderstanding still appears, most likely in two places. The first is with students and their new-found tools. One of my students was getting into trouble because he always ran to the teacher with every little problem. I told him that for some of the small things he should try a "do-it-yourself" approach. The next day he belted Roger in the mouth and proudly announced to his teacher that he was only doing what I had told him to do. What we have here is a failure to understand! The misunderstanding could have been compounded had the teacher taken the child literally. The teacher's knowledge of the PBM Plan and its goals, however, can prevent an overreaction. The PBM Administrator must endeavor to show the student how to use the tools to best advantage.

Some students will still exaggerate, but problems can be avoided with knowledge.

The second point of misunderstanding is with parents. The PBM Administrator must be something of a diplomat. Because of this, some parents misunderstand what you are trying to tell them. They take this misunderstanding with them when they talk to teachers or building administrators. One parent caused me some trouble when I said to her, "I'm doing the best I can to help your son, but unless he tries harder, some of us will lose patience." What I was trying to tell her was that we would have to devise some solution to her son's problem using the techniques mentioned in Chapter 11. This parent, however, stormed into the principal's office wanting to know why the teachers didn't have as much patience with her son as the PBM Administrator did. However, that is not what I meant. Making certain that parents understand what you are telling them will avoid explaining your motives to administration and faculty. If they understand what you are doing, it is possible for them to explain to parents, and communication is again restored.

HOW TO GAIN FACULTY SUPPORT

When I began the program I found what I called the 1/3 ratio. I was starting a *new* program oriented toward the handling of behavioral problems, and about a third of the faculty was solidly behind me. The Program was new, and they would have been behind it no matter what I did. Another third was sitting on the fence; they were undecided. They were not too sure that this was the way to handle it, but something had to be done. They were watching me, and they could go either way. The final third was the most difficult. They were unalterably opposed not just to me, but to the Program and the "waste of money" as they considered it. Since the Program worked with the class disruptor, the one who was causing the most problems, it seemed to them but another example of the "bad student" getting the attention while the "good student" was left by the wayside. That third was the most difficult to convince. It is from this source that the faculty support problem comes.

As the Program progressed, I found that the ratio, or support formula as I called it, broke down to 3/5:2/5. While 2/5 of the faculty were still opposed or leaning against the Program, 3/5 were actively supporting it. By the time the Program had been in effect from four to six months, the ratio further changed to 9/10:1/10; 9/10 now supported the Program, some actively and some passively, while 1/10 remained opposed. That 1/10 was the most vocal and the sector I had to work with most cautiously. Even though I had picked up support from many of the original 1/3 opposed, this final 1/10 would never be able to support the Program. They thought so, they said so, and they acted accordingly.

Tread lightly with this 1/10. The Program itself must do the showing and explaining for you. They must come to accept it on their own. One way in which the PBM Administrator can help is by always asking their advice and by keeping very close communication with them.

Johnny, for example, has been giving everyone problems. Johnny is now in the Program. One faculty member, Mr. James, just can't stand Johnny. Mr. James can't see that the Program is going to do Johnny any good except to pamper him. If I were to go to Mr. James and say, "Look, you're doing something to Johnny or he's doing something to you that is throwing him off for the rest of the afternoon. I'm going to find out what it is, and then I'll tell you how to avoid it in the future," Mr. James would probably throw *me* out of the room. An argument might ensue in which, while there might be a winner, Johnny would be the loser.

It would be more effective if I asked Mr. James' opinion on something I had already thought out. If Johnny always misbehaves in the afternoon, perhaps I should say, "Mr. James, perhaps if I saw Johnny for a few minutes before he came to your class after lunch, we might be able to find some way of handling him. What do you think?" I would make sure that once I had tried this option with Johnny, I would keep checking back with Mr. James to see if it was working. Mr. James then would be actively involved in the Program and might feel that he was at least partially responsible for the outcome.

PRACTICAL METHODS OF OVERCOMING RESISTANCE

There are other points of resistance. The person who runs the program, for example, seemingly has extra free time. The PBM Administrator may not be in the PBM Room as often or as long as teachers are with their classes, but the time spent out of the room is often as productive as the time spent in it. You may be in the Teacher's Room, walking the halls, or popping into classrooms, but there is a reason for this: you are gathering information and observing behavior for use in the Program. This, however, is easily misunderstood by teachers who are busily working and trying to find just a few spare moments to do their lesson plans.

Also, there is a great deal of confidentiality or secrecy between the student and the PBM Administrator. Indeed, there may be things the child tells you which may never be repeated. Because of this, some teachers may feel that the students are talking about them behind their backs, and that the information gathered may in some way be used against them. The explanations on confidentiality previously given, however, should alleviate this notion.

Guidance counselors sometimes feel that the PBM Administrator is infringing upon their professional responsibilities. After all, aren't they the ones who are supposed to deal with the students' problems? In Chapter 10, the PBM Plan in relationship to the guidance personnel within a school is outlined. The PBM Plan does not usurp or take over any guidance duties, but is a valuable extension and asset to this valuable service.

Should school psychologists feel that you are entering their area or practicing psychology without a license? Of course not. Again, Chapter 10 relates in detail how invaluable one school psychologist found the PBM Plan. Indeed, she expressed to me her feelings that the Program allowed her to most effectively utilize her expertise with students who could most benefit. To her, the PBM Plan was a highly valuable tool.

Because they run the school, administrators must be in touch with everything that happens. When a child comes to see you, however, it may be a "spur-of-the-moment" thing. The administrator does have the right to know where any given student is at any given time; however, the PBM Plan must also be accessible to students. If I were to tell the administrator every time Richie came to see me, it might hamper Richie's use of the program; but this conflict can be resolved: try to get a message to the administrator as soon as possible. Abstracts also keep administrators informed. Moreover, I set up a schedule whereby I met with the administrators every Friday morning at 9. In this way all decisions are discussed, and the administrators feel they have control over the events in their building.

Teachers, guidance counselors and building administrators as well as the PBM Plan are all working for the same purpose— the social, emotional and educational growth of the student. If there is resistance on the part of any of these, the only practical method for overcoming it is patience, understanding and the assurance that all are partners working toward a common goal.

REPORT FROM THE "BATTLE ZONE"

Since its inception, many valid questions have been raised concerning the PBM Plan. In this section, the questions most frequently raised are presented in question-and-answer form.

Why do you feel that the PBM Plan is so much more effective than the present options for controlling behavioral problems?

The PBM Plan is more effective for two reasons. First, everybody is an individual, and the current options do not recognize this. Even if two students get into the same behavioral difficulty, they do it for different reasons. Personalized Behavioral Modification is individually oriented: each child is treated differently because each child *is* different from any other. The second reason is the unique parental involvement which the PBM Plan sponsors. Constructive, positive contact with parents seems to be out of fashion in recent times. While the PBM Plan may not save the family structure, it at least recognizes the home as an extremely important part of the child's development and education and strives for home involvement.

> How can you be certain that the PBM Plan can adapt to all schools in all locations with varying socio-economic and cultural backgrounds?

While there is a basic design to the structure of the PBM Plan, that is, a four-step approach, analysis of patterns, self-worth reinforcement, etc., the individual tools for change find their roots in the individual child's background. Hence, they are geared to *that* child alone, whatever his background. Furthermore, each school selects its own PBM Administrator. Hopefully, that Administrator is of similar background to the students involved in the program. For example, a PBM Program in a predominantly black, inner-city school would most likely have a black PBM Administrator who can relate to the students.

> You claim that you wish to destroy all forms of stereotyped thinking. Isn't using your grid to pinpoint a child's problem just another type of arbitrary categorizing?

If you look at the grid you will notice that the divisions pertain to the *viewing* of a behavior. If it is arbitrary to select the 25 or 30 that have occurred over and over and over again, then it is; but as to stereotyping a child, this is untrue. Based on what the *child* says, the divisions merely indicate how the individual child views a particular situation. Two incidents involving the same child may be different. The grid helps me locate the precise tools for an individual, but only in relationship to his individual thinking. To stereotype is to prejudge actions or thoughts. This is never done!

If, as you claim, you separate work and behavior, what
justification do you have for handling an academic problem in
basically the same manner you would a behavioral problem?

Separation of academic difficulties and behavioral problems occurs primarily in the use or nonuse of punitive options.
There is, however, a correlation in the patterns that lead to
either academic weakness or failing to meet socially acceptable
norms of behavior. A child who consistently forgets to do
homework and another who misbehaves in class both need tools
for successfully changing their patterns of behavior. The tools
given to reinforce the need for homework may be similar to the
tools used by a student to avoid misconduct. Patterns of failure
are changed to patterns of success.

You set very high standards for the PBM Administrator. Didn't
you ever lose your temper or yell at a student?

Oh, yes. I am a volatile person and I have a temper. I think
I can honestly say, however, that I never lost my temper with a
student *personally*. Now that is not to say that I didn't get
extremely angry with some of their behavior. I think injustice
and stupidity can make me fly off the handle faster than
anything else. When I encounter one of these situations, you
most likely can hear me. But consider: I get angry at the
behavior, not at the child. The child has dignity and worth: it is
his behavior that leaves something to be desired and needs
changing.

If the PBM Plan is so dynamic, what keeps "good" students
from misbehaving just to get into the program?

That has not been my experience. Every student, even the
"good" ones, sometimes has problems he or she wants to talk
over. PBM is always available to all students; students don't
have to "be bad" to get to talk to the Administrator. Consequently, the "good" students don't have to misbehave to gain
recognition.

Isn't involving the parents in the PBM Plan just another public relations tool?

Definitely not! Parents have always been interested in what their child does in school. The PBM Plan merely reinforces the understanding that the school is interested in what the parents think. In many cases, parents' help is essential to successfully change a pattern of behavior in a PBM student; parents play a real part in the process. Granted, positively involved parents will talk about the school in positive ways, so good public relations may well be a by-product, but parental involvement for the benefit of the child is the primary PBM goal.

With the personalized attention given to each student, the forms to be filled out, the abstracts, the parent conferences, and all the other activities of the PBM, how can one person attend to all these duties in a school day?

The answer is simply that all these activities do not take place in a single day. With a little planning and careful record keeping, one person *can* handle it all. There are some parts of the PBM Plan that can be scheduled, while others can't. If a child is placed in the PBM Room, the PBM Administrator must remain with him. Use this time for things that can be done at the desk. If there is no one in the room, use this time to gather information and deal with activities that take place outside the room. Not everything has to be done at the same time.

When the PBM Plan is evaluated, how can you be certain that it is the program and not the PBM Administrator who is being evaluated?

The PBM Administrator and the Plan itself are indeed connected. How well the PBM Administrator understands and uses the techniques of Personalized Behavioral Modification will really spell the success or failure of the Program in an individual school. The Program is a series of practical techniques—the PBM Administrator is the technician.

> In trying to change the behavioral patterns of a child, aren't you actually delving into psychoanalysis?

No, and we don't see how it can even be construed that way. A mother who advises her daughter or a father who is engaging his son in a "heart-to-heart" talk in order to help him is not practicing psychoanalysis. They are using good common sense coupled with experience and a genuine, heartfelt desire to help. This is what the PBM Administrator does. That's not psychoanalysis—that's caring!

> Why should a school system select the PBM Plan over any of the other behavioral modification programs that are currently being offered?

The answer lies in the basic differences between the PBM Plan and all other types of behavior modification programs. First, the others use some external method to effect the change—either a special class, a special environment, or something that in some way sets the individual student apart and outside the mainstream of school society. The PBM Plan disagrees with this concept of changing the environment to change the behavior. The real world outside of school does not allow for "special environments." Rather, the PBM Plan maintains that students must learn to adapt *their* behavior to adjust to their environment. Reality remains the same. PBM is a *real* plan for dealing with *real* situations in a *real* world.

Moreover, with the PBM Plan you don't have to wait until "something happens" for the plan to go into operation. In fact, one of its most attractive features is the preventive nature of the Plan. Actually, many behavioral difficulties are avoided entirely because the "trouble spot" is reached *before* the trouble occurs.

Finally, the "Personalized" aspect of PBM is extremely dynamic. All too often, our schools reflect our increasingly impersonal society. The student is a number, a level, a reading score, an aptitude or potential. He is not Steve Anderson, whose favorite color is blue and who wants to go to Wisconsin to see cows. PBM treats each child as an individual, and in so doing it turns Metropolis into Smalltown, U.S.A. In the "big city" you are a statistic, alone in the midst of many, alienated—it is not yours. In Smalltown everybody knows your name, and you know other people; they *care* and consequently, you care about them, their lives and their property. Smalltown is yours, and you don't destroy what is yours. This is one of the best reasons for selecting the PBM Plan.

Appendix A

Testing Your Effectiveness as PBM Administrator

The following is a fictionalized case study. It is accompanied by several questions in which you are required to play the part of a PBM Administrator. By answering these questions and then checking your results and interpretations with the answers given in Appendix B, you should get a pretty good idea of the rationale and workings of the PBM Plan.

The lines of the case study are numbered in order that specific references may be made in Appendix B.

Are you ready? O.K., let's go!

JANUARY 16 – 10:31 a.m.

1	Wayne Lawrence is brought to the PBM Room by the vice-	1
2	principal. Wayne carries some books with him. The vice-	2
3	principal signs the Administrative Discipline Sheet and	3
4	leaves the boy standing there. There are two other students	4
5	in the room, one taking a test, and one who has been	5
6	referred for yelling in class.	6

Question 1:

What is the first thing you would do with Wayne?

7	After reading the Administrative Discipline Form,	7
8	you discover that the vice-principal wants Wayne to re-	8
9	main in the PBM Room for the rest of the day. You take	9
10	two forms from your desk.	10

Question 2:

What are these forms, and what do you do with them?

11   Assuming at this point that you are ready to begin   11
12   the first interview, you have the proper form in hand,   12
13   and you either have the grid memorized or in front of you.   13

Question 3:

What is the first question you ask?

14   Assume that Wayne crosses his arms and replies, "I   14
15   don't see what all the fuss is about!"   15

Question 4:

What is the next thing you say?

16   In reply Wayne says, "Oh, Mr. Johnson got all upset   16
17   just because a couple of us were talking!"   17

Question 5:

What is your next question, and how are you recording the answers?

Question 6:

As a preliminary decision, where would you place Wayne's reasons for his behavior?

Question 7:

Having completed the interview, what do you do?

18   You fill out a Teacher Report Form and have it sent   18
19   to the teacher involved.   19

JANUARY 17 – 9:00 a.m.

20   Wayne is back in class and no students are scheduled   20
21   to be with you until the conference you have scheduled   21
22   for 10:15 a.m.   22

Question 8:

In reference to Wayne, how can you be occupying this hour?

JANUARY 17 – 10:10 a.m.

23   The principal sends you a note requesting your pres-   23
24   ence *as soon as possible* to talk over an impending parent   24
25   conference.   25

Question 9:
    What do you do?

26   Back in the PBM Room, you jot down a few notes on Wayne   26

27   and file them.   27

       JANUARY 18 — 10:35 a.m.

28   Wayne arrives for a scheduled conference.   28

Question 10:
    List the procedures for the conference.

Question 11:
    Given information you have gathered, Wayne's attitude, and any new information gathered during the conference, devise two tools you might give Wayne based on your analysis.

Question 12:
    Using you own analysis of the situation again, when (if you decide to) would you schedule another conference for Wayne?

       JANUARY 23 — 1:30 p.m.

29   You are called to the office to collect Wayne from the   29

30   principal. He is creating a disturbance, being abusive,   30

31   and generally acting enraged.   31

Question 13:
    What procedures do you follow?

32   The principal has suggested that Wayne's parents   32

33   should be involved.   33

Question 14:
    How would you go about it?

Question 15:
    What are some of the procedures you might use to get one or both of Wayne's parents into school?

34   Resulting from this latest incident, Wayne has been   34

35   assigned to the PBM Room for two days.   35

Question 16:
    When would you schedule a discussion with Wayne, and what would be some of the points of this discussion?

Question 17:
What would you *not* say?

Question 18:
When would you schedule Wayne for the next conference?

JANUARY 26 — 11:03 a.m.

36	Wayne's mother arrives unscheduled and upset, having	36
37	misunderstood the tone of a letter sent home with Wayne.	37

Question 19:
What do you do?

38	Following the discussion with Wayne's mother, points	38
39	of agreement are reached. A plan to try and aid Wayne is	39
40	worked out between the two of you. Toward the end of the	40
41	parent conference Wayne is called, and a three-way confer-	41
42	ence takes place to the satisfaction of all parties.	42

Question 20:
What are some procedures and techniques you might use to
help Wayne to change his pattern of behavior successfully?

MARCH 18 — 1:54 p.m.

43	Wayne has stayed out of difficulty and most confer-	43
44	ences have been satisfactory. Parental involvement has	44
45	been consistent, and a marked change in attitude has	45
46	been noted.	46

Question 21:
Would you release Wayne?

Question 22:
What would you use to aid you in your decision?

Appendix B

Evaluating Your Results

Here is your chance to evaluate the test offered in Appendix A. We have attempted to analyze both the case study and the questions. Specific line numbers of the case study are referred to, and specific page references are included to verify the evaluation or to seek further information. We hope you will find it helpful.

The mental picture of Wayne Lawrence may not be the same for all readers, but the questions were phrased to allow for creative analysis while strenuously adhering to PBM principles.

Here we go!

JANUARY 16 — 10:31 a.m.

Lines 1-6

Nothing is known as the student enters (pp. 79-80; 115-116). The setup of the room would place the two children on opposite sides of the PBM Room. You would place Wayne near the student who had been referred for yelling in class (pp. 36 and 38). From the books in his hand you deduce that he has left a class and that the teacher will have to be notified (pp. 47-48). The reasons for Wayne's referral have been left up to your imagination, but let us assume it was for classroom distraction.

Question 1

We would suggest you have Wayne sit down. There is nothing to indicate that he is in an emotional state, so normal entrance procedures into the PBM Room are possible (pp. 38-39).

Lines 7-10

The length of time Wayne will be in the room overlaps more than one class period (pp. 93 and 96).

Question 2

The two forms are the Student Schedule Form and the Referral Sheet for Disciplinary Action (pp. 153-169). You would notify his teachers and gather assignments as quickly as possible (pp. 93 and 96).

Lines 11-13

An assumption is made that you have cleared your desk, announced that a conference is about to take place, and the rules of the room are noted (pp. 40-41).

Question 3

Use the procedures for the use of the grid. You say, "What did you do to be sent here?" (pp. 55-59).

Lines 14-15

Keep in mind the *reasons* for frequent student misconduct (pp. 47-48).

Question 4

Be sure to cut off further discussion quickly with the question, "Why are you here?" (pp. 55-59).

Lines 16-17

This answer strongly indicates that Wayne's reason is rebellion (pp. 47-48). According to the grid, his answer shows an indication toward peer acceptance (p. 58).

Question 5

Your next statement would be, "I wasn't there. Describe what happened." (pp. 55-59).

The incident was left to your imagination, but let us assume that Wayne told you a story relating the incident that he and his buddies were just having fun in class. The teacher couldn't get them to stop, so he dismissed Wayne because the teacher thought he started it. Wayne did nothing wrong; it wasn't his fault. He was just fooling around with his pals (p. 58).

You are recording the answers in an anecdotal style on the Referral Sheet for Disciplinary Action (pp. 105-106; 152; 171).

Question 6

Wayne is there for class distraction (according to our description of the incident) with some overtones of rebellion, and it appears that his basic reason is the acceptance of his peers (p. 47).

Question 7

You would tell Wayne that he is to report for a conference in two days at a specific time. By now, his assignments should have arrived from his teachers (pp. 74; 168). If not, set him to work with the book he brought with him and indicate what seat he is to take (pp. 36 and 38).

Lines 18-19

Using the procedures as outlined in this book, remember to observe confidentiality, take note of the way the story is being transported to the teacher, and take steps to avoid resistance (pp. 152; 168-170; 188-189).

JANUARY 17 – 9:00 a.m.

Lines 20-22

This is an example of spaces of time which become available for information gathering techniques (p. 55). Be sure you are aware of the possible pitfalls of "free" time (p. 188). Do not forget to check your daily schedule (p. 152).

Question 8

Some time could be spent gathering pertinent information preparatory to the conference (pp. 117-119).

Lines 23-25

This one is tricky. *Nothing* prevents a conference taking place when scheduled (p. 60). Even though you will have to see the principal, nothing can be accomplished in five minutes. Furthermore, you need a few moments to prepare for that 10:15 a.m. conference.

Question 9

Set the appointment with the principal at the end of the 10:15 conference, explaining the reason (pp. 108-109).

Lines 26-27

You are starting a file on Wayne which now includes an Administrative Discipline Report Sheet, a Referral Sheet, a file card, a Student Schedule Form, and a carbon copy of the Teacher's Report Sheet (pp. 153-169).

JANUARY 18 – 10:35 a.m.

Line 28

This is done with the use of the Conference Pass. The class he is to come from is at approximately the same time as the original incident. You should have a Conference Report Sheet before you, and you have briefly reviewed Wayne's file to refresh your memory (pp. 117; 153-170).

Question 10

At many points in the text, this has been spoken of both as a Preventive Conference and a conference after a Referral. (See Chapter 4, pp. 54-65; 80-84; 98-99.)

Question 11

This requires that you use your imagination. You may draw upon the examples we gave, or perhaps devise some of your own. The important thing is that they be based on both Wayne's apparent reasons and reasonings for his behavior (pp. 60-62).

Question 12

This, too, would have to be based on your imagination, but we caution you that a conference too soon is better than a conference too late (pp. 62; 83).

JANUARY 23 – 1:30 p.m.

Lines 29-31

Keep in mind that Wayne is now a part of the Program. The principal may be upset and angry, but Wayne is *referred*, not suspended. You may be called upon to argue this point (pp. 84-85; 92-93; 103-104).

Question 13

Your handling of Wayne would be according to the principles of a second Referral. Also, at this point you could begin checking for patterns. Please note that there are seven days from incident to incident. This may be significant (pp. 80-81).

Lines 32-33

It is a perfectly reasonable request. Let's assume, just for this analysis, that you had not contacted Wayne's parents after the first incident. You may have decided to do just that (Chapter 11, pp. 138-149).

Question 14

All contacts with parents are made with the understanding of the child (139-141).

Question 15

Parental contact can be handled according to certain procedures, but remember that each set of circumstances is different and each parental contact should be handled as unique (pp. 144-146).

Lines 34-35

Here, particularly, the continuation of Wayne's education must be handled smoothly. Use all procedures, contacting teachers, and gathering assignments. *This is not an In-School Suspension.* It does, however, have the same inherent problems (pp. 182-184).

Question 16

The discussion should be held toward the end of the second day to prepare Wayne for his re-entry into class. Even though the second referral procedure was followed when he first entered the room, *this* discussion should have the aspects of a concentrated Preventive Conference. The aim of this conference is to start the child's analysis of his own behavior (pp. 98-99). Emphasis should be placed on any successful adjustment of behavior Wayne showed from January 17 to January 23 (pp. 62-63).

Question 17

This is a most crucial point. You do not make any
references to the fact that Wayne has failed, has misused the
tools you suggested, has gained your disapproval, etc. This
support, even when it appears they are "bad," has a most
dramatic effect on most students (pp. 59; 79-80; 119-120;
133).

Question 18

Even though Wayne has not been on an In-School Suspension, he has been away from the social aspects of the school
for two days. Positive reinforcement should be handled
quickly, as close to the start of the school day as possible. See
Wayne on his first day back (9 a.m. on January 25).

JANUARY 26 − 11:03 a.m.

Lines 36-37

View this as a blessing in disguise, not as a time to get
defensive. The parent *is* in the school (pp. 139-146).

Question 19

Procedures for handling the parent, regardless of his or her
emotional state, are vital to the eventual successful outcome of
the child's involvement in the PBM Program (pp. 139-148).

Lines 38-42

There are several points of interest here:
1. You have actively enlisted the aid of the parent (pp.
   142-146).
2. The robe of confidentiality extends over them both.
   You need not tell one what the other said (pp.
   140-141).
3. Your priority is Wayne. When he enters, the situation
   must be explained to him, and he must agree to take
   part. If he does not, set it up for another time (pp.
   140-141).
4. All parties have a stake in the outcome.

Question 20

The main point here is to set up a Preventive Conference
Schedule for Wayne. If there are indications of academic

weakness, consider using the Academic Achievement Factor. Given this imaginary student and his attitudes, consider involving him in a Self-Worth Reinforcement project (pp. 121-122).

MARCH 18 — 1:54 p.m.

Lines 43-46

Note should be taken of the fact that from six to eight weeks have passed since the initial involvement with the PBM Plan. Various techniques have been tried and there are obvious indications of Wayne's success.

Question 21

Consider this decision well. Aside from choosing the best tools to help Wayne, this is the most important decision you will make on his behalf (pp. 84-85).

Question 22

Assuming that your records on Wayne have been kept up to date, you have three points to consider:

1. Wayne's progress as shown through past conferences and teacher comments (pp. 84-85).
2. The Student Evaluation Sheet (Figure 6-1, p. 86).
3. The present evaluations of his teachers and parents as to his progress (pp. 84-85).

These, combined with your own observations, will show you how well Wayne has adapted to socially acceptable norms. If all indications are favorable, release Wayne and count him as a success for the PBM Plan and for you.

Finally, if the techniques described in this book have helped you as a teacher in your classroom, have helped you as an administrator in your school, or have helped one student to realize his full potential, to turn him on to learning, and to set him on the pathway to start becoming a human being of worth and dignity, then it indeed has been worth the effort.

Index